ABOUT THE
STARMONT READER'S GUIDES TO CONTEMPORARY
SCIENCE FICTION AND FANTASY AUTHORS

The past two decades have seen an enormous upsurge in the interest in science fiction and fantasy. It is rare to find a bookstore that doesn't now prominently feature brightly colored examples of space and magic. It is unusual to find a high school, college, or university that doesn't offer at least one science fiction or fantasy course. Most significantly, it is becoming increasingly difficult to meet someone who hasn't succumbed to the lure of these two entertaining literatures. The Starmont Reader's Guides were created to satisfy the needs and interests of this varied readership. Bringing together acknowledged authorities, the series offers a thorough examination of each author; indeed, many of these efforts represent the first time the authors have been examined in book form. Each volume is divided into a chronological table of the author's life and literary career, a full biography, chapters on the major works or groups of works, and both primary and secondary bibliographies. Without sacrificing the sophistication that each author creates in his or her fiction, they clearly and cogently explore and explain the important issues, providing depth and understanding for both the beginning and the sophisticated reader.

It is hoped that the Starmont Reader's Guides will be of value to the student, teacher, librarian, scholar and fan by contributing to our understanding of the many authors and fascinating works that have provided us all with so much pleasure and insight.

Dr. Roger C. Schlobin, Series Editor
Department of English

DR. ROGER C. SCHLOBIN is currently an Associate Professor of English at the North Central Campus of Purdue University. He is co-editor of "The Year's Scholarship in Science Fiction and Fantasy," which appears annually in *Extrapolation;* one of the authors of *A Research Guide to Science Fiction Studies*; and has written *The Literature of Fantasy: An Annotated Bibliography of Fantasy-Fiction* as well as the bibliography of the works of Andre Norton.

FRANK HERBERT

STARMONT READER'S GUIDE 5
DAVID M. MILLER
Series Editor: Roger C. Schlobin

Starmont House ▪ P.O. Box 851 ▪ Mercer Island, Washington 98040

Library of Congress Cataloging in Publication Data

Miller, David M.
    Frank Herbert.

    (Starmont reader's guide ; 5)
    Bibliography: p.
    Includes index.
    1.   Herbert, Frank—Criticism and interpretation.
I.   Series: Starmont reader's guide to contem-
porary science fiction and fantasy authors ; 5.
PS3558.E63Z77   813'.54   80-20880
ISBN 0-916732-16-9

DR. DAVID M. MILLER is Associate Professor of English at Purdue
University. Among his publications are *The Net of Hephaestus* (1971),
John Milton: Poetry (1978), and several articles on the fiction of J.R.R.
Tolkien.

This book is for Erik and the garage.

CONTENTS

I

GENERAL INTRODUCTION AND EVALUATION

—A beginning is the time for taking the most delicate
care that the balances are correct— (*Dune*, p. 9).

From first (*Under Pressure*, 1956) to current last (*The Jesus Incident*, 1979), the novels of Frank Herbert form a remarkably unified treatment of two complementary problems: 1.) If man does not achieve a balance within himself and with his environment, existence is merely a version of chaos. 2.) If man freezes an achieved balance, decadence sets in and life yields to entropy. Thus the problems to be solved by Herbert's characters require that chaos be organized and stasis disturbed. The desideratum is dynamic homeostasis.

Homeostasis is the tendency of an organism to maintain a uniform and beneficial physiological stability within and between its parts. If we extend this definition to include not only biological organisms but also psychological, social, economic, political, religious, and ecological units, and if we subject that expanded homeostasis to a universal evolutionary imperative, we have a nutshell version of Herbert's themes.

But themes do not make fiction until they are given form: articulated in action, embodied in characters, set in space and time, and allowed to validate themselves in the reader's perceptions. The range of forms into which Herbert shapes his dominant themes is broad: the organism to be balanced (or disturbed) ranges from a four-man submarine to the entire universe; contending forces may be embodied in a small boy and a crazy Indian or they may inform the pan-sentient population of the cosmos; interest-devices range from lab-report vampire-gauges to sentient stars; plots are sometimes simple, sometimes complex, and sometimes merely complicated; characters may be as wooden as Harvey Durant, the "father" in *The Eyes of Heisenberg*, or as empathically rounded as Duke Leto, the father in *Dune*; sometimes we see the action from the plotters' perspective (*Dune Messiah*), sometimes from the perspective of the plotted-against (*The Heaven Makers*). Herbert's modal range is also wide: *Under Pressure* is extrapolated realism; *Whipping Star* is a playful nightmare fantasy. *Soul Catcher* is neither science fiction nor fantasy; *Dune* is both. Many novels have a strong odor of detective fiction (*Under Pressure, The Santaroga Barrier, Hellstrom's Hive*). The *Dune* trilogy has strong affinities with sword-and-sorcery fiction.

The relationship between Herbert's pervasive double theme and the form in which that theme is set forth also varies. Sometimes the problem seems to be an excuse for action, adventure, and suspense. Sometimes the tale exists to articulate the problem. Books of the first kind may be called *entertainments*; books of the second kind may be called *essays*. Entertainments depend upon substitutions within well-established formulae. Essays depend upon variations upon generally understood models. A good book, not to mention a great book, must be both, for authors ought still to be in the business of delighting and instructing. When the entertainment sketches a new formula, when the essay invents a new model, the result is no longer "popular" fiction, although such books are frequently very popular indeed if they succeed in establishing the revised formula and stretched model as a new standard. Herbert has achieved such revision and stretching only once (so far).

Dune is, by almost any standard except perhaps that of deconstructionist fiction, a remarkable book. The essay that Herbert seems driven to write and rewrite is, in *Dune*, marvelously iterated, embodied in each link of a chain of being, reaching from the cell to the universe. The entertainment weaves the formulae of fantasy and science fiction with quest, ritual, maturation novel, melodrama, and tragedy. Perhaps the most remarkable aspect of *Dune* is the concrete plenitude of Arrakis, the desert planet. It has become a critical platitude of speculative fiction that strange characters having strange adventures in strange places is at least one too many stranges. In *Dune*, Herbert's ability to create a "real" fictional world through copious representative detail, analogies to our primary world, and through the use of patterns drawn from the "reality" of our other fictional worlds provides firm grounding for even so unnatural a creature as a sandworm. And the world of the Fremen is as tangible and tactile as the exotic lands we met as children in old copies of *National Geographic*. Without elevating a coincidence to causative status, the careful reader may note that there appears to be a correlation between the fullness with which Herbert renders his fictional world and the quality of his fiction.

In the review-essays which comprise this introduction to Herbert, I sometimes judge works harshly. All of his fiction is entertaining, much is thoughtful, and some is very fine. That *Dune* is Herbert's second published novel, that its two sequels are less satisfactory, and that each Herbert book now carries some version of "a great book by the award-winning author of *Dune*" must abrade Herbert-artist even as it delights Herbert-businessman. Herbert does seem trapped; not only because dynamic homeostasis as a theme can have no end, but also, perhaps, because the bread-and-cheese habit demands rapid writing; hence, formula fiction. *Soul Catcher* seemed a genuine effort to break free from the pattern, but *The Dosadi Experiment* goes back to formula, even though it is "bolder" in language and "sexier" in scene. *The Jesus Incident* reads like a crisis; *Destination: Void, The Godmakers, The Green Brain* are all in there, but so is Cordwainer Smith and Harry Harrison, and maybe even Stephen Donaldson's *Chronicles of Thomas Covenant* (1977). Herbert's next book may indicate some fundamental decisions on his part.

Since Herbert is currently working on a movie of *Dune*, perhaps he will go back to his trilogy, write the whole thing again (from back to front), and so make a fine work into a masterpiece.

This introductory study has no room for many things that ought to be said of Herbert's fiction. Chiefly, a good deal of work needs to be done on his sources, allusions, and topicality. For spice, read "oil" and Iran comes into focus. "Orange-Catholic" is Irish humor. Agamemnon was an Atreides. If this study aids readers and prompts critics, it will have accomplished its purpose.

My chief indebtedness is to Frank Herbert. But I also thank his wife, Beverly, for supplying chronology and biography. My wife, Joanne, helped mightily with the bibliography, and all who work in science fiction will continue to owe William Contento for his detailed *Index to Science Fiction Anthologies and Collections* (G.K. Hall: Boston, 1978). Since I do so little with Herbert's short fiction, perhaps my bibliography will encourage others to trace the development of theme and skill as Herbert plied his trade in the pulps.

Finally, if you disagree, or want to say "Yes, but . . .," or feel compelled to point out things I have misssed, go ahead. Write me a letter.

David M. Miller
Department of English
Purdue University
West Lafayette, Indiana
47907

II

CHRONOLOGY

1920   October 8, born, Tacoma, Washington. Parents: Frank and Eileen (nee, McCarthy).

1940   Married Flora Parkinson, San Pedro, California (divorced 1945).

1941   United States Navy.

1942   Daughter, Penny, born, February 16, San Pedro.

1946   Attended University of Washington.
         June 23, married Beverly Ann Stuart.

1947   Son, Brian Patrick, born. June 29, Seattle.

1951   Son, Bruce Calvin, born. June 26, Santa Rosa.

1956   *Under Pressure (The Dragon in the Sea)*

1964   *Dune World* serialized in *Analog* (December, 1963, January and February, 1964), nominated for a Hugo Award.

1965   *Dune* wins Nubula Award for Best Novel.

1966   *Green Brain*
         Destination: Void
         Eyes of Heisenberg
         Dune wins Hugo Award for Best Novel.

1968   *The Heaven Makers*
         The Santaroga Barrier

1970   *Dune Messiah*
         Whipping Star
         New World or No World
         The Worlds of Frank Herbert

1971   *The Godmakers*

1972   *Soul Catcher*

1973   *The Book of Frank Herbert*
         Hellstrom's Hive (Project 40)
         Threshold

1975   *The Best of Frank Herbert*

1976   *Children of Dune*

1977   *Children of Dune* nominated for Hugo Award for Best Novel.

1978   *The Dosadi Experiment*

1979   *The Jesus Incident*

198?   *Direct Descent*

198?   *Priests of Psi* (to be published in England)

198?   A computer book, untitled, with Max Barnard

198?   *Dune*, a $40-million-dollar movie

III

BIOGRAPHICAL FACT SHEET

Vital Statistics: Born October 8, 1920, Tacoma, Washington, to Eileen Mc-Carthy Herbert and Frank Herbert, Sr. Married Flora Parkinson, 1940, San Pedro, California; one daugher, Penny (Mrs. D.R. Merritt, three sons). Married Beverly Stuart, 1946, Seattle, Washington; two sons, Brian Patrick (married Janet Blanquie, two daughters) and Bruce Calvin. One sister, Patricia (Mrs. Roy Larson). Presently lives on Olympic peninsula in Washington State.

Education: Tacoma, Washington, and University of Washington, Seattle. Military photography training. Special research and study in psychology, arid lands, photography, ecology, alternative energies, education.

Profession: Newspaper reporter and editor in Glendale, California; Salem, Oregon; San Francisco and Santa Rosa, California; Portland, Oregon; Tacoma and Seattle, Washington.

Published: Twenty-three books in print, nineteen in the field of science fiction. Best known works: *Dune, Dune Messiah, Children of Dune.*

Awards: Hugo, Nebula for *Dune*

IV

NOVELS

Under Pressure, the first of Herbert's published novels, is the mildest of science fiction: there are no space ships, no bug-eyed-monsters, no buzz words, no travels through time, no aliens, and the occasional blackboxes are limited to plausible extensions of current technology.

The action is set in the near future, after an atomic war has left the world divided into armed and tactically warring camps. The enemy is threatening, but not demonic, and the heroes are quite aware that their problems are mirrored in their antagonists: war is hell, and everyone is simply doing his duty as it is presented.

The representative microcosm is a four-man subtug, *The Fenian Ram*, which sneaks to the enemy continental shelf, steals crude oil, and tows it home in a mile-long bladder. The overall crisis of the war has its corollaries in each facet of the novel: the sea is malevolent, the equipment fails, the skipper is schizoid, the first officer is an emotional cripple, the engineering officer an enemy sleeper, and the recent communications officer completely mad. The universal tension is epitomized by the atomic power plant of the submarine; without it, the submarine is lifeless, but at every moment it threatens to kill the crew with its life-sustaining radioactivity. The sea, the sub-base, and the submarine are constantly spoken of as wombs, signaling the heavily psychological orientation of the novel. Thus, the specialization of the hero, undercover man for the Bureau of Psychology (BuPsych), is inevitable.

Ensign Ramsey is sent to the *Ram* to analyze the failing homeostatic balance of the captain, the crew, the sub, the sea, the war—and by implication—the world. With Ramsey, we discover that dynamic tension is tending toward chaos, that the tenuous flow-permanence is failing, and that the evolutionary imperative of life has stalled. We have in *Under Pressure* one side of Herbert's ubiquitous coin; however, were the problem reversed, were homeostatic tension yielding to the smoothly ordered stasis of entropy, Ramsey would be from BuSab. (*The Green Brain* [1966] is an examination of entropy's dangers, as is *The Dosadi Experiment* [1977].)

To achieve his goal, Ramsey must become an integral member of the crew, yielding his "individuality" to the life-sustaining collective. Each exciting crisis serves as an initiation rite for Ramsey; each danger forces him into closer contact with himself, and when the danger is mostly past, he curls up, catatonic, in a fetal position. When he uncurls, he is reborn as man-plus, able to read minute signals in his fellows and himself, aware of the symbiosis that makes the crew more than the total of its members, and cognizant of the solution of the *Ram*'s (other subs', the world's) problems. The solution is about as satisfying as "cottage-cheese." Ramsey decides that all the submariners need to make them happy is recognition, brass bands, and higher pay. The triviality of the "answer" is also a mark of Herbert's fiction; since the problems he raises are perhaps unanswerable and since a book *has* to end, most of his endings seem circular, or contrived, or simplistic, or all three at once. Perhaps the most profound answer Herbert here gives to "life" is right out of Joseph Conrad: sanity is the ability to swim and the willingness to grab an oar when it is offered.

The characters of *Under Pressure* are versions of the cast that populates Herbert's fictional world. Their interrelationships are based upon variations in the nuclear family: father-son, uncle-nephew, brother-brother. Women are strictly for shore-leave: nubile, pneumatic, and "nympho," though there are mild hints of Herbert's uneasy relationship with his female characters in the rank-conscious secretary and the allusions to the cuckolding captain's wife.

Herbert's ability to construct a concrete secondary universe in which to set action in motion is vividly evident. One could build, from the details Herbert includes, a scale model of the *Fenian Ram* (just as we might make a stillsuit from *Dune*, or trace the strange journey in *Soul Catcher* on a map of our western mountains).

The plot of *Under Pressure* moves from one crisis to the next, but the there-and-back-again of the quest and the incremental repetition of initiation rites save it from episodic-picaresque. Major characters come through intact with the exception of Garcia, and his death is payment for past debts and a release from his unwilling perfidy. Ensign Ramsey is off to bigger and better things, Bonnett is ready for his own command, and Captain Sparrow can start again with a new crew.

Major Characters:
> Ensign John ("Long John") Ramsey, brilliant, redheaded undercover man from BuPsych.
>
> Commander Harvey Aston Sparrow: Captain of the *Fenian Ram*, father-figure who has adjusted to the insane world of his subtug.
>
> Garcia: "Britished" Latin engineering officer, unwilling enemy sleeper.
>
> Lieutenant Commander Leslie Bonnett: Psychologically flawed by childhood trauma, unhealthily dependent upon Sparrow.
>
> Dr. Richmond Oberhausen: Director of BuPsych; blind mentor of Ensign Ramsey.
>
> *Fenian Ram*: four-man subtug.

Dune

Once in a great while "entertainment" and "essay" blend through the conventions of popular literature into the major concerns of a generation of readers; J.D. Salinger's *Catcher in the Rye*, William Golding's *Lord of the Flies*, J.R.R. Tolkien's *The Lord of the Rings*, and Robert A. Heinlein's *Stranger in a Strange Land* are such works. The success of such works is not a matter of "literary" excellence (though a degree of excellence is necessary), nor is it a matter of articulating an ideological, philosophical, or moral stance (though the works of which I speak do so). A book, like a painting, may be "right" or "wrong" in ways that usurp prescriptive formulae, enliven platitudes, and transform stock characters into something like archetypal manifestations. The price of generational success can be very high: teachers and academic critics feel displaced and resentful. And when another generation comes along, the extravagant claims of fans who are no longer young may even serve as a barrier to understanding and evaluation. Although I was captured by each of the works I have listed during its moment, *Catcher* now seems bumptiously adolescent, *Lord of the Flies* seems something of a melo-dramatic allegory, and *Stranger* seems so carelessly written that I can't even reread it. *The Lord of the Rings*, however, holds my interest after twenty readings. Perhaps it is the depth of its world in topology, in history, and in values that makes the difference. Perhaps it is the frankness of admission of fantasy. Perhaps it is the solid, time-tested symbolic structure; perhaps the parallels to atemporal, collective wishes and fears; perhaps the easy skill of narrative voice makes us believe that the author believes.

Although *Dune* has not yet proven that it belongs on the same shelf as *The Lord of the Rings*, whenever I am asked that aching, fearful question, "Are there other books like Tolkien's?" I answer, with careful caveat, "Try *Dune*."

* * *

Most of Herbert's novels seem designed to be read once; hence, story lines are clear, there is little parallel action, genre markers are unequivocal, and proleptic clues are relatively obvious. Such is not the case with *Dune*, for Herbert's masterpiece is essentially a series of overlays. The first page tells us that we are entering a gothic novel: "Castle Caladan . . . the ancient pile of stone . . . bore the cooled-sweat feeling it acquired before a change in the weather." And sure enough, down a "vaulted passage" comes an "old woman," "a witch shadow—hair like matted spiderwebs . . . eyes like glittering jewels." But the gothic "half-light" is cast by a science-fiction "suspensor lamp." Paul is trained in weapons suitable to a young Lancelot, but he duels an auto-mated opponent and wears a force shield. The "gom jabbar" is an ancient poisoned needle, but the device that tortures his hand is a technological marvel, quite literally a black-box. Sword-and-sorcery clues mix with gothic clues and science-fiction clues. Yet the background is as cleanly lighted as Hemingway's fiction. The "mysticism" of Hesse merges with the meticulous combats of C.S. Forster. The exposition required to establish the fictional world is ponderous, yet excitement and suspense seldom lag. Much of *Dune* is overtly didactic, yet the "lessons" arise from plot, character, and action. The satirical applications to our primary world are obvious, but only on reflection. Allegorical conflicts between reason and intuition, between masculine and feminine, between good and evil, between earth-rapers and ecologists, between individual desires and social imperatives, between morality and politics are at the service of character, plot, and action. All this is to say that *Dune* is a novel that invites the reader in, rather than a novel that intrudes upon the reader. In this sense, it is "escapist." If we must label it, "epic fantasy" is perhaps least misleading; but it is epic fantasy without a god, the tale of a hero who unwillingly devours his helpers, a conquering of time and place by a superman who is but the tool of genetic diaspora. We may more profitably acknowledge that *Dune* really fits none of our categories, although it has the markers of many.

16

The primary narrative voice never breaks from the dramatic present, never seems to know more than either the characters or the reader; hence, the tales unfold without a hitch because the narrator is as interested as are we in what will happen next. Paul may not survive the gom jabbar, may smother in the sand, may be killed by Jamis, may die in the melange trance, may be killed by Feyd-Rautha. But the head-notes to each section tip the hand. The opening paragraph tells us that the Harkonnens are ultimately symbiotic; the biographical head-note on Yueh tells us that he will successfully betray Duke Leto, and so on throughout the book. Clearly Paul is going to make it to the end or there would have been no head-notes.

An illuminating exception to this practice occurs as we return to the Harkonnen heir, Feyd-Rautha. Princess Irulan's headnote, rather than being narratively proleptic, is grandly sententious: *"The concept of progress acts as a protective mechanism to shield us from the terrors of the future"* (p. 330). The chapter that follows is a "bull fight" with an Atreides' captive playing the bull to Feyd-Rautha's matador. The bull almost wins, would have won had Feyd played according to the Atreides Code. Yet the suspense yields to fate, for Herbert's primary narrative voice opens the chapter with: "On his seventeenth birthday, Feyd-Rautha Harkonnen killed his one hundredth slave-gladiator in the family games" (p. 331). Even when Herbert "slips," he maintains a basic strategy of providing the reader with an outline to be filled in by narrative detail. We neither know, nor much care, who Princess Irulan is until very late in the novel. Yet her function is important, for her head-notes allow Herbert to make the comments he wishes to make to guide understanding without disturbing his "companion" contract with the reader. Further, we "know" the actions happen, because Irulan tells us they have happened before we see them happening. When we at last discover that Irulan is Paul's wife of political convenience, barred from the bed and relegated to the study, the "historical" head-notes are welded tightly to the plot, a happy choice by Herbert for many reasons. Although Herbert sometimes manages a similar irony with the headnotes of volumes two and three (as when Harq al-Ada is discovered to be Fard'n), the later books are less careful in maintaining the proleptic displacements.

The proleptic dreams and increasingly frequent prescience of Paul serve, narratively, a similar function. The reader is told ahead of time what will happen so that, when the event occurs, it seems both "right" and real. And when Paul is overwhelmed by cellular fate, the loss of control is the more devastating in that the reader is also deprived of security. Thus, Herbert is able to make the events of the novel seem both inevitable and spontaneous.

This effect is reinforced by obvious, almost mechanical, parallels in adversary relationships. Turn the Atreides upside down and you have the Harkonnens. Chapter one establishes Paul, Hawat, and Leto; chapter two sets up Feyd-Rautha, Piter, and Baron Harkonnen: matter for a conventional melodrama. Whatever the Harkonnens have done, the Atreides will do the opposite: animals versus humans. But when we learn that Jessica *is* half-Harkonnen and that the Old Duke and the bull that killed him are tightly linked in the Atreides code, the black-and-white dichotomy of melodrama yields to the complexity of something like yin-yang.

These brief examples are characteristic of the dynamic tensions of the whole book: Herbert *uses* many of the conventions of entertainment fiction, but he is not, in this case, *used* by them. The result is neither strange nor familiar. I think my grandchildren will like *Dune*.

* * *

Much of the complexity and depth of Herbert's secondary universe in the *Dune* series derives from an elaborate system of power structures; hence, a good question with which to begin is "Who's in charge?" Ultimately the answer is "No one," but several organizations think that they control both tactical and strategic flow. One may think of the power structures as a system of overlays, each level of which believes that it is using all the others.

Dune's universe is—on the overt, "official," level—feudal. All planets belong to the emperor. But, just as in Earth's history, problems of logistics, transport, and communication modified the theoretical power of a feudal king, so is the emperor's power modified. Various "cousins" (real and honorary) of the emperor are granted planets in fief, which in fact often become hereditary possessions. Such Dukes and Barons are, in day-to-day matters, absolute monarchs. Collectively, their power is greater than the emperor's, and so the emperor's primary political duty is to foment rivalries among the nobility to prevent a serious challenge to the throne. Any partial challenge can be fought off by the emperor's Praetorian Guard, the Sardaukar.

But the efficiency of the emperor's private army encourages the very alliances he fears. The official structure of alliance among the nobility is the "Landsraat," a parliament of Houses Major and Houses Minor. The ultimate fear of any noble is that the emperor will isolate him from the herd and loose the Sardaukar upon him. Yet any noble alliance is destroyed by internal jealousy and rivalry. Vacancies in the nobility are filled by clever, ruthless men who amass wealth and establish new houses. The Atreides and the Harkonnen are again exemplary: the Atreides are an ancient house, actually related to the emperor; the Harkonnen are middle-class interlopers. The enmity between the two houses is partially one of class, though a Harkonnen ancestor has been banished by an Atreides ancestor for cowardice. The Harkonnen envy the noble Atreides; the Atreides disdain the merchant Harkonnen. It's the old game of rock, scissors, and paper.

The framing action of *Dune* is set in motion by a major, Imperial, political ploy. The Harkonnen are getting too rich as slave-masters of Arrakis. Leto Atreides is valorous, generous, loyal—a man so honorable that his men follow him out of love. Both houses pose a threat to the emperor, but the Atreides' threat is the greater, for the emperor is without a son. Duke Leto is obvious emperor material, and he has an heir. In one stroke the emperor hopes to dislodge the bloated spider and destroy the shining hero. Nice move. The perfect ploy is to eliminate the Atreides by appealing to their code of honor. And the "Old Duke" has provided an exemplum: as the bull to Paul's grandfather, so is Baron Harkonnen to Paul's father. In both cases, the virtues of the Atreides can destroy them.

The feudal power structure, however, is somewhat anachronistic, for power no longer flows inevitably to the brave, the good, or the kin. As in the late Renaissance, money, not land, has become the bottom line. Thus the economic arena is where the real battles are settled, and that arena is manifested in a huge, interplanetary corporation. CHOAM (Combine Honnete Ober Advancer Mercantiles) provides the board-room for wheeling and dealing. Everyone, including the emperor, competes for director chairs and voting stock. It is the emperor's task to play the same divide and conquer game in CHOAM that he plays in the Landsraat.

The size of the Imperium, however, has spawned a group of specialists who comprise yet another layer of power. Transport from solar system to solar system is necessary, or the whole, elaborate structure will collapse. And all inter-system transport is in the hands of the Space Guild. Nothing and no one moves between star-systems except in Guild vessels. Thus the Guild would seem to hold the trump card, ultimate power over all the contending factions. But the Guild's ability to move ships faster than light depends on prescience, for they must know where they are going before they get there, and only knowledge of the future makes faster-than-light movement safe. Guild navigators gain prescience by taking large doses of an addictive drug, melange (spice), and spice comes only from the planet Arrakis, Dune.

In summarizing the power structures, I have described a closed ecology, in unstable equilibrium. The Imperium depends upon the Landsraat, the Landsraat upon the Imperium. Both draw economic power from CHOAM. CHOAM cannot function without the Space Guild, but the Space Guild is dependent upon spice. Since spice comes only from his majesty's desert planet, the emperor remains in charge but only by playing Machiavelli on a tightrope. Everyone conspires to keep the system in balance and at the same time tries to destroy the system by surpassing everyone else. Clearly spice is the key, not only because it enables the transportation necessary to permit power, but because it is a genuine geriatric. Thus it preserves both the system and the individual. The recipe is one designed to produce endless conflict, from bickering to double dealing to "Kanly" (ritualized feud) to guerilla war. But no one can afford full-scale war because real war would cut off the supply of spice.

The particular shuffle of reality that has produced the current situation is the Butlerian Jihad, a revolt against computers that resulted in the religious command: "Thou shalt not make a machine in the likeness of a human mind." Out of that chaos came not only the major structures I have detailed but three significant "service" organizations. To replace the computers, *Mentats* were developed, men trained to process information as a super-computer might. All the major power brokers need a mentat to guide their machinations. But mentats remain men; hence, their loyalty must be secured. Again the Harkonnen mentat, Piter, and the Atreides mentat, Hawat, represent the spectrum of control. Hawat follows the Atreides because he loves them. Piter serves the Harkonnen because he fears them and yet hopes to satisfy his unspeakable lusts by increasing Harkonnen power. Both Hawat and Piter are also trained assassins.

The second "service" class is the *Bene Gesserit*, all women as the mentats are all male. Young Bene Gesserit, like young mentats, are sold to important men. But the B.G. are sold as concubines, wives, or (in rare cases) truth sayers who can instantly judge the truth of any statement. Bene Gesserit depend upon highly developed *gestalt* awareness, and their reading of minute signals enables them to exercise total psychological control. To their detractors, they are "witches," whose voices can shred a man or whose sexuality can reduce him to putty. They also have perfect control of their autonomic nervous systems, of their emotions, and of their musculatures. A successful politician needs both a mentat and a Bene Gesserit. The homosexual Baron Harkonnen has no Bene Gesserit.

The third class of specialists—which is not much developed in the novel—is medical. In a Borgia world of poison and intrigue, a man must be able to trust his doctor. The *Suk Doctors* are given imperial conditioning that makes their Hippocratic oaths unbreakable. The only Suk we meet is Yueh, the "oriental" Atreides physician whose conditioning has been broached by the Harkonnen. Yueh is eternally in love with his Bene Gesserit wife, and the Harkonnen have kidnapped her: wheels within wheels.

Each group of specialists is supposedly obsessed by its calling, but the thinking machine mentats have time to love and hate, and the Bene Gesserit are infintely more than male-dominated willowy maids, fecund matrons, and wise crones. What, after all, can stand against the power of the bed, the delivery room, and the confessional?

Bene Gesserit power is such that they actually constitute a shadow government of the universe; for, unlike Imperium, Landsraat, CHOAM, Guild, and Mentat, the Bene Gesserit do more than play tactical *realpolitik*. They have a selfless purpose. In spite of their acknowledgment that what the human race really desires is a genetic diaspora (an orgy of uncontrolled gene mixing), the Bene Gesserit have for centuries been running a eugenics program. Their current power is developed not only by disciplines, but because they are guided by *reverend mothers* who have, through poison, joined the collective memory of all their female ancestors. The male memories, however, form a black hole in the collective unconscious from which they flee in terror. Their plan is to breed, selectively and amorally, for a male reverend mother who would possess complete racial memory, both male and female. Thus, Bene Gesserit wives and concubines are sterile or fecund according to the breeding chart; the preferred Bene Gesserit pattern is to continue important blood lines only in females whom they control.

As the reader of Herbert's other novels might expect, such "selfing" is not the way to produce an optimum. Progress will require the union of contraries far more complex than any chart can display. At the same time, the Bene Gesserit program is a necessary, though not sufficient, factor in the fate of humanity. Perhaps only a male reverend mother could have sufficient power to upset the many layers of entrophic structures that are winding down the genetic spring.

As fate would have it, the emperor's power game has chosen the same two families that the Bene Gesserit breeding program has been developing. And Jessica's violation of the program in producing a son, rather than a daughter, gives Duke Leto a reason to accept the emperor's gambit of Arrakis: he wishes to secure a permanent place of power for his son, Paul. Jessica's fears for Paul have led her to have him trained as both Bene Gesserit and mentat. Later, the desert and the Fremen add to Paul's combat training to make him a super-Sardaukar. (Selusa Secundus, the boot camp for Sardaukar, is a country club compared to Arrakis.) The self-serving mumbo-jumbo sowed by the Bene Gesserit's "missionaria protectiva" against future crisis has, under the pressures of Arrakis and with the help of spice, grown into a full-blown messiah myth. Thus Paul becomes everything: mentat, Bene Gesserit, reverend mother, duke, and "Mahdi" (the one who will lead us to paradise). With the added religious horsepower, one Freman Death Commando can eat a dozen Sardaukar before breakfast and exclaim, "Fie on this quiet life, I want work!"

Paul's "uncontrollable purpose" is to father the jihad necessary to remix the human gene pool. He can defeat all minor contrarieties, but each victory is precisely what is needed to insure his final defeat. *Dune* is remarkable in that all this macro-action bumps along in the margin as a very real human being struggles against real, incrementally deadly, tactical difficulties.

*   *   *

The central tale that orders and focuses the satisfying complexity of Herbert's secondary universe is the maturation of Paul Atreides: a skinny, fifteen-year-old boy evolves into the Emperor of the Universe. Paul is a "psi-focus" (*The Godmakers*), a fulcrum upon which the macro-organism of sentience teeters in the imperative process of maintaining dynamic homeostasis. As in most of his fictions, Herbert's fundamental metaphor is the closed ecological system. Paul is typical of Herbert heroes in that he seeks to control forces which constitute him. Each episode in his growth illustrates a paradox: like a virus, Paul devours his family, his friends, his tutors, his testers, his enemies, and all the antagonistic symbioses which make the universe go around. But he is also like a vaccine: the universe absorbs Paul, readjusts its metabolism, and makes the disease a defense. Strategically Paul is more victim than victimizer, for his "terrible purpose" uses him more dispassionately than he spends his death commandoes. Yet he maintains his humanness, even at the cost of the jihad he abhors: he leaves the final metamorphosis to his son, Leto II, and dies a human being on the steps of Alia's temple (*Children of Dune*). Paul-messiah is, finally, only John the Baptist; for the human chrysalis triumphs, returning its water to the tribe. In a nutshell, Paul sacrifices his godness to the Atreides code; Leto II, as we shall presently note, is a god at the price of his humanness.

From a macro-perspective, Paul is like everything else: the river remains, each water molecule passes on to the sea. When a mentat ceases to function, the master buys a new one. When Jessica refuses to produce a daughter on command, Countess Fenring seduces Feyd-Rautha. When the Fremen reverend mother dies, her memory passes to Jessica. Always the evolving structure remains, passing from one dynamic equilibrium to another. (Perhaps Herbert's vision owes a debt to Olaf Stapledon's *Last and First Men*.) Yet for the narrative to succeed in the face of fate, some freedom of significant action must remain, and Herbert risks that significance by equipping Paul with prescience.

A great deal might be said of Herbert's essay on the relationships between past, present, and future—between foreknowledge and free will—only to wind up in endless mazes wandering lost. Here, it must suffice to note three ways in which Herbert saves the freedom of entertainment without destroying the fixity of essay. The probing of a prescient mind into the future masks the probed areas from other prescient minds (*Dune Messiah*); the act of prescience involves the Heisenberg uncertainty principle: touching the future with one's mind alters those elements which are touched; and prescience thrusts upon the seer potential, rather than absolute, futures. Curiously, when Paul (*Dune Messiah*) succeeds in living his past memory of the future in the present, the effect—because the memory unfolds sequentially—is that of a relatively minor miracle: a blind man sees. And the reader is neither surprised nor shocked because Irulan's head-notes have given the reader a kind of prescience—the reader can share even greater prescience by reading the book a second time.

Paul is a *human* hero because he maintains a corner of self. His sister, Alia, is *unhuman* because she does not maintain such a corner—although Herbert allows her a tiny space to choose death (*Children of Dune*). Thus Herbert's definition of humanity demands a strong sense of self riding on species consciousness. Both Paul and Alia are eddying vortices that gather strength from resistance, break established channels, and spew the jihad and the religion of Dune in tidal wave across the universe. The vortex may grow to whirlpool, to maelstrom, to Kralizec typhoon. The wheeling focus may last perhaps 5,000 years (Leto II). Yet the clash of vortex and river can have but one conclusion: when resistance ends, the vortex fades and the river flows on to the sea, altered, but still the river.

*   *   *

The action of *Dune*, and to a lesser extent of the two other volumes, is punctuated by a series of incremental, ritual initiations. Each ritual serves to unify two or more contending forces in the person of the initiate, forming a complex unity which he carries into the next ritual: thesis, antithesis, synthesis; thesis[2], antithesis, synthesis[2]. And so on. We enter the series in *medias res*; Paul has been trained in disparate disciplines: mentat (male) and Bene Gesserit (female). (Farad'n of *Children of Dune* is given only Bene Gesserit training.) Thus Paul's early training prepares him to be androgynous, for his mother pursues the Bene Gesserit goal: to breed a Tieresian Kwisatz Haderach who will have access to both male and female genetic memory. The eugenic effort has been going on for centuries, but the water of life has proven mortal to all would-be reverend mothers. Count Hasimir Fenring has come closest, but he (a male Bene Gesserit, though not a reverend mother) is a congenital eunuch, rather than an androgyne.

A second synthesis is that of animal and human. This thesis and antithesis is sited in Paul's two grandfathers: the Harkonnen-animal Baron, the Atreides-human Old Duke. For grandfather and father Atreides, the attempted synthesis has proven mortal. Likewise their adversaries, bull and Baron, are destroyed by the consequence of killing humans. Herbert plays a rich, touch-and-go game with the bull fight metaphor. The Atreides portrait of the Old

22

Duke and the head of the bull that killed him reappear on the walls of the Harkonnen palace as we see the animal-Feyd play matador to a human-Atreides bull. Paul's ritual slaying of Feyd draws the bull fight to a close by distinguishing human from animal: unlike Feyd who kills his gladiator with the aid of a subconscious paralysis keyed by the word "Scum," Paul refuses to use the disabling Bene Gesserit implant. Alia has already disposed of the Baron, a bull no longer brave, though his memory spirit gains revenge by possessing her (*Children of Dune*).

Each of the rituals that led up to the slaying of Feyd draws power from two contradictory-complementary sets of psychological symbolisms. Freudian-sexual symbolism asserts the white pain of isolated individualism: its effect is to heighten tension. Jungian-archetypal symbolism soothes the individual consciousness by asserting the place of the one within the many: its effect is to relieve tension. When combined, the two sets of symbols can produce dynamic-stasis: a tightly coiled spring that resonates without vibration. The Bene Gesserit litany against fear enables the individual to join with his contrary and yet remain an individual. In each of Paul's ritual testings, overtones of Oedipal sexuality yield to Jungian sexual individuation: Baron Harkonnen has perverted this power into homosexuality; Count Fenring has escaped into asexuality. Both Count and Baron have enormous, but incomplete, power. Paul has more. Leto II has all. Of the four, only Paul maintains his humanity. Count and Baron fall below, Leto II passes beyond the human.

Here, it is only possible to assert, to exemplify, and then to pass on. The gom jabbar ritual testing of Paul, which opens *Dune*, is repeated in many keys and modes throughout the novel. The initial gom jabbar ritual certifies the triumph of Atreides human genes over Harkonnen animal genes, marks the first of several rituals that move Paul from boy to man, and establishes the Oedipal tension that spreads musk over Paul's crises. Herbert's touch, though fairly delicate, is obvious. The witch-mother places a death-phallus at Paul's neck, forces him to thrust his hand into a dark box. The hand is burned away through intense pain, and emerges, reborn. Later, that hand seizes the death-phallus hunter-seeker, which slips into Paul's bedroom, just in time to save another witch-mother, the Shadout Mapes. This time, Paul smashes the phallus, rather than merely escaping.

Meanwhile, Jessica—who has undergone the Bene Gesserit gom jabbar when the winds of puberty tortured her flesh—has herself been tested by the Shadout Mapes whose gom jabbar is a tooth taken from the vagina dentata of a maker's mouth. When Jessica and Paul are trapped in the 'thopter with two Harkonnen assassins, Jessica's sexuality loosens Paul's bonds, and Paul kicks the assassin through the heart. When Jessica and Paul share a tent buried beneath the sand, Jessica feels "reborn" as they emerge. When Jessica is buried in a sand slide, Paul fishes her out and pronounces the word that brings her back from bindu-suspension. Together they pull the fremkit, which gives them life in the desert, out by its umbilical strap.

Paul never quite escapes the tensions of sexuality, for he takes revenge on his mother, vicariously, in two ways: when he silences Gaius Helen Mohiam with threat of a death word and when he forces Irulan to marry him without ever entering his bed. Thus, he defeats the triple power of the Bene Gesserit.

The maid is confined, the matron is made barren, and the crone is emasculated. Chani, his mate, has no formal claims upon him, and the attraction between them is much like that of brother and sister. When he finds his sister, Alia, flushed and naked from duelling with a lethal automated pel, it is she who is sent to a cold shower (*Dune Messiah*). The "pharaonic" marriage of brother and sister is achieved in *Children of Dune* when Leto II and Ghanima wed, though Leto's metamorphosis prevents it from being consummated.

The other side of the coin—the slaying of father—marches, symbolically, through the same rituals in which Paul moves from "female" threatened with penetration to male who penetrates. (The match with Feyd does the male-female role ambivalence very obviously in terms of death rape.) As the symbolic structure provides Paul with several mothers, so it also provides him with a number of fathers. Leto is the first to be supplanted. When Paul sees his father tired and afraid, some of Leto's "fatherness" dies. When, at the water banquet on Arrakis, Paul moves to fill his father's empty chair. Kynes steps in as father-protector. Liet-Kynes also plays Baptist to Paul's Messiah, just as Paul plays Baptist to Leto II's Messiah: both must die to make way for the savior.

On Caladan, Paul has had the benefit of a number of surrogate fathers, most of whom die to give Paul skill and space. Duncan is the first to die, Hawat the last. Yueh is an interesting case in that he serves Paul doubly: by "killing" Leto and by saving Paul—shades of Hamlet and Claudius. Gurney is faced down by Paul as he is about to kill Jessica, and he (*Dune Messiah*) becomes Jessica's man in unspecified but suggestive fashion. Paul's training echoes of the education of King Arthur. Hawat makes Paul a mentat, Gurney makes him a musician, Duncan makes him a great swordsman, and Yueh gives him an Orange Catholic Bible. Since each father is something more than an allegorical figure, their gifts overlap, but the pattern is clear: specialists produce a poly-man.

On Arrakis, Paul finds two additional fathers: Liet-Kynes and Stilgar. Both are seduced by the Atreides honor, and although Kynes' sacrifice is the more obvious, Stilgar's is the more profound. Kynes dies for Paul, Stilgar lives for him. Kynes' daughter, Chani, becomes Paul's sister, then his lover, then his concubine. Stilgar offers to marry Paul's mother, fathers Paul by naming him Usul, offers himself to Paul's knife; but his greatest sacrifice is to remain himself, diminished beneath Paul's growing shadow. When Stilgar takes Paul's rejected *ghanima*, Harah, as wife, the sexual symbolism of dominance evidences their relationship. In a curious way, Jamis also fathers Paul into the Fremen tribe, and the cost to Paul's fathers is, here, explicit. Jamis loses his life, his water, his baliset, his wife, and his children—even his "coffee" service—to Paul. The souls of his fathers are but more grist for Paul's mill. If Baron Harkonnen is a carnivore, Paul is an omnivore, and his food seeks him.

The final confrontation scene draws all the power threads into a single knot and summarizes Paul's victory. By seizing the power to destroy the source of melange—and evidencing the will to do so—he has the Guild, the Imperium, CHOAM, the Landsraat, and the Bene Gesserit by the throat. But since he is unwilling to surrender his humanity, he remains vulnerable. He has promised Chani sons, and thereupon hang two more tales.

Major Characters:

Atreides
>Old Duke: father of Leto I, killed by a bull.
>Leto I: father of Paul, accepts Arrakis as planet in fief, killed by Baron Harkonnen.
>Paul: hero of *Dune* (also called Usul, Muad'Dib), welds Fremen into fighting unit, beats all comers, becomes emperor.
>Jessica: Bene Gesserit concubine of Leto I, Paul's mother.
>Alia: Paul's younger sister, born after Jessica's reverend mother transformation; adult at birth; kills Baron Harkonnen.

Atreides Retainers
>Duncan Idaho: dashing swordmaster.
>Thufir Hawat: mentat assassin.
>Gurney Halleck: warmaster, musician.
>Wellington Yueh: Suk doctor, traitor.

Imperial Family
>Shaddam IV: emperor, House Corrino, fathers five daughters, among them Irulan (Paul's wife) and Wensicia (Farad'n's mother: Corrino heir).
>Count Hasimir Fenring: Shaddam's cousin and friend, assassin.

Imperial Retainers
>Gaius Helen Mohiam: Bene Gesserit reverend mother; truthsayer for emperor.
>Liet-Kynes: Royal ecologist, goes native on Arrakis, father of Chani
>Aramsham: Captured Sardaukar.

Harkonnen
>Baron Vladimir: gross, evil father of Jessica; mortal enemy of Leto I
>Count Glossu Rabban: "Beast Rabban," brutal governor of Arrakis; nephew to Baron Vladimir.
>Feyd-Rautha: favorite of Baron; rival and foil of Paul.

Harkonnen Retainers
>Piter: mentat assassin.
>Iakin Nefud: guard captain.

Fremen
>Stilgar: Fremen leader who takes in Jessica and Paul.
>Shadout Mapes: house servant to Jessica.
>Liet-Kynes: ecologist, Fremen leader who plans transformation of Arrakis.
>Chani: daughter of Liet-Kynes, Paul's concubine.

Jamis: hotheaded Fremen; Paul's first slaying.
Harah: Jamis' wife, inherited by Paul.

Dune Messiah

When Herbert decided to continue the *Dune* epic, he faced a number of interesting possibilities. The jihad, begun on the last page of *Dune*, could have provided a vast space-opera of Paul's Fremen flooding the universe. The growth of the Harkonnen seed in Countess Fenring's womb could have continued the Atreides—Harkonnen double saga. *Dune Messiah*, however, is not a repetition but a continuation, and it is the fourth of a five part work, as well as the second volume of a trilogy. Theme, not character or setting or action, is the focus; and so Herbert skips the twelve years of jihad, leaves the Harkonnen *in utero*, and watches the teetering of Paul's empire now that the "terrible purpose" of genetic diaspora has been accomplished.

The theme is familiar: what are the relationships of power, of time and eternity, of chaos and entropy? What is the nature of "freedom"? The answers are also vintage Herbert. A man may ride a sandworm for a time, may even guide its course, but his only real choice is to get on and then get off. To stay with power is to be absorbed by it. The third section of *Dune* is "Prophet," and after prophet comes messiah. But Paul is not necessarily the Messiah of the title. In book one, Paul proved that he was human, not animal; now, he must test the other extreme of humanity: is he human, not god? The head-note of chapter one sets an hypothesis: "There exists no separation between gods and men; one blends softly casual into the other." The same is true of animal and man, yet a man may choose, even if the choice destroys him. The testing of the proverb begins with a flurry of invention that expands the complexity of *Dune's* power structures.

At the far edges of the universe, man's reach has gone beyond the limiting orthodoxy of *Dune*. The Ixians build technological wonders in defiance of the precepts of the Butlerian jihad—we hear little about them. Of the Tleilaxu, however, we learn a good deal. In defiance of "nature's" ways, the Bene Tleilax have blended the principles of giving and taking, of male and female into their hermaphroditic selves, and they have extended *prana-bindu* control of muscles and nerves to the ultimate. Their "face dancers" are perfect chameleons, able to mime so well that they sometimes lose themselves in the performance. The Tleilaxu have built, rather than bred, a kwisatz haderach; and when he proved uncontrollable, they have, almost casually, led him to commit suicide. However, the Tleilaxu, like the Chem (*Heaven Makers*) and the Optimen (*Eyes of Heisenberg*), are bored. The guild has also moved beyond the bounds of *Dune*: their master navigators are fish-like humanoids who swim in tanks of melange gas.

Paul's reshuffling of power structures presents the Tleilaxu with the opportunity for an experiment. From the flesh of Duncan Idaho, they have grown a ghola and equipped it with mentat and Zensunni training. Hayt, as the revenant Duncan is called, is perfectly Duncan in all respects save one: he lacks the "soul" of the original. The Tleilaxu sell the ghola to the guild as a weapon against Paul. They hope that the stress of loyalty will bring Duncan's soul back into Hayt.

Paul's refusal to follow the carnivore instincts of his Harkonnen genes has kept him from extirpating his enemies: the Padishah line, the Bene Gesserit, and the Space Guild. Yet if he is to continue as emperor, he must domesticate all three. The Tleilaxu send a face dancer, Scytale, to play in the dregs of ruined ambition. Reverend Mother Mohiam yet claws after the genetic cross embodied in Paul and wishes to recapture the female power seized by Alia. Edric, the Guild Navigator, hopes to secure control of the spice necessary to his existence. Irulan, Paul's Padishah consort, wants a number of things: to bear Paul's heir, to fulfill her Bene Gesserit mission, and to restore the dominance of her father's line. As in *Dune* each conspirator hopes to use all the others. The Tleilaxu really don't care how it all comes out so long as they can play god.

The plot that occupies the foreground of *Dune Messiah* is marvelously complex, a testimony to the incompatibility of the conspirators. Even the central thrust, the destruction of Paul, is not shared by Irulan who is the liaison between the plotters and their quarry. Paul is to be given a series of paradoxical choices. The first step is to offer him Hayt-Duncan. If he accepts the gift, he has taken a murderer into his household; if he refuses to succor a faithful retainer, he has violated the Atreides Code. The second step is to administer a contraceptive drug to Chani so that Paul's need for an heir will force him to impregnate Irulan. If he abandons Chani, he is false to his code; if he fails to produce an heir, he is false to his role. The third step is to foment revolution among the Fremen. If Paul fails to suppress the revolt, he will lose his empire; if he suppresses the Fremen, he will destroy the culture that has nourished him.

So far, the plot looks pretty good; in each case Paul is damned if he does and damned if he doesn't. But there are also contingency plans. If Chani conceives and dies in childbirth, the ghola's murder compulsion will be triggered. If Hayt resists the compulsion, he will either self-destruct or really become Duncan Idaho. If Hayt kills Paul, the Tleilaxu will offer to bring Paul back as a ghola in return for Alia's surrender. If he does not kill Paul, the Tleilaxu will offer to bring Chani back to life in return for Paul's abdication. As with his father and grandfather, Paul is to be trapped between losing and becoming that which he abhors.

This Byzantine plot is superimposed on the difficulties inherent in Paul's own situation. The kanly between Atreides and Harkonnen lies fallow in Allia's genetic memory. The Fremen are falling apart, either to be swallowed by their own religious bureaucracy (like Korba) or to chew on the memory of the good old days (like Farok). Paul's promised paradise stinks, both in the desert and in the plush ghetto reserved for old death commandoes. Paul's major strength, prescience, is disrupted by the Dune Tarot and by the meddling of Space Navigators so that both he and Alia must take near lethal doses of melange to see the future. He has his own destructive paradox: without prescience he cannot ride power; but prescience destroys freedom, and without freedom he cannot be human.

Dune Messiah differs from *Dune* in a major way: Paul swirled through the plots in *Dune* as he rose to the top: the plots in *Dune Messiah* swirl about his knees as he looks down from great height. A major lever of science fiction, sympathy for the underdog, does not operate in *Dune Messiah*. As with *Whipping Star*, much of the entertaining action is irrelevant to the essay theme. When the plotters get close enough to Paul to throw their nets, they are themselves enmeshed. Paul sends a knife through Scytale's brain. Duncan kills the dwarf, Bijaz. Stilgar kills Gaius Helen Mohiam. Alia condemns Korba and Edric to death. Irulan finds herself devoted to raising the children of Chani who have dispossessed her line.

Despite the complexity of plot, only three actions are thematically significant. Paul accepts Hayt-Duncan; Paul knowingly walks into range of the stone burner; Paul rejects the Tleilaxu offer of a revenant Chani. Each choice is the same choice. Paul refuses to become a god as he earlier refused to remain an animal. *Dune Messiah* might be summarized as the love story of Paul and Chani: "It was mostly sweet, but you were sweetest of all." *Dune Messiah* is, perhaps, Herbert's strongest argument for resisting the forces that move man to violate humanness. The true human always knows when to get off the sandworm, and in that descent finds triumph. Paul's initial gom jabbar ritual has proven permanent; in his case, at least, the proverb about gods and men is disproved. A man, not a god, walks into the desert as the book ends.

But in the desert lie two Atreides heirs who know all about taking and giving, who have already passed the water of life, who have perfect genetic memory. Ghanima and Leto are a double kwisatz haderach. Their creche contains the god that Paul refused to become, and the twins must soon be about their father's business. *Children of Dune* will be the story of what happens when a human does not get off the sandworm.

Major Characters added to the cast of *Dune*:

Plotters Against Paul

Scytale: Tleilaxu Face Dancer; puppet master of plot

Gaius Helen Mohiam: Bene Gesserit, Reverend Mother, Imperial truth sayer

Edric: Guild Steersman, fishlike, prescient

Irulan: Paul's wife, daughter of Shaddam IV, wants a son by Paul

Farok: Fremen malcontent who desires old days

Korba: Priest of Alia's temple

Ghost of Baron Harkonnen: takes possession of Alia's psyche to gratify his lusts and destroy the Atreides

Hayt: revenant of Duncan Idaho; Alia's lover

Bijaz: dwarf made by Tleilaxu, human distrans, trigger for Hayt's killer conditioning.

Friends of Paul

Alia: Paul's sister and high priestess of his religion (see Ghost of Baron Harkonnen above).

Chani: mother of Paul's twins

Duncan Idaho: breaks through out of Hayt

Children of Dune

Children of Dune is in several ways more of a piece with *Dune* than was *Dune Messiah*. The focus is once again upon a child rising, rather than upon an adult falling. *Dune* is a comedic *Bildungsroman; Dune Messiah* is an epiphanic tragedy; and *Children of Dune* is a "divine" comedy in which the hero transcends both the success of victory and the failure of defeat. *Children* is more carefully written than *Messiah*, less dominated by the contrivances of "plotting," and, because Leto's significant action is *acceptance* (as opposed to Paul's *rejection*), more in tune with the thematic thrust of Herbert's fictions. In some ways, *Children* is the happiest excursion Herbert makes into his obsessive concern: the nature of human consciousness. The random shots at defining consciousness quoted, below, from *Destination: Void* are here subdued to plot, character, and action. That Herbert should have, most recently, been led to co-author a sequel to *Destination: Void* (*The Jesus Incident*) is understandable for both commercial and thematic reasons, but Herbert might have been better served to make *Incident* a sequel to his *Dune* world, rather than to the Ixian-Tleilaxu world of *Void*. The relationships between Ship-god and Leto-god are obvious, but their origins are antithetical: *Ship* is the product of ignoring the lesson of the Butlerian jihad: "Thou shall not make a machine in the image of a man's mind"; Leto is the product of ignoring the lesson of Paul's jihad: "Thou shall not suffer thy humanness to be lost."

As he begins *Children*, Herbert gives us a description of his narrative method:

A spot of light appeared on the deep red rug which covered the raw rock of the cave floor. The light glowed without apparent source, having its existence only on the red fabric surface woven of spice fiber. A questing circle about two centimeters in diameter, it moved erratically—now elongated, now an oval. Encountering the deep green side of a bed, it leaped upward, folded itself across the bed's surface.

Herbert is at his best when the light seems independent of its source, when it is focused on the bed rock of human consciousness, and when it encounters, rather than creates, that which it reveals. Simply put, Herbert is better at Jung than at Freud, better at taking us to a secondary universe we have within us than at creating an alternative reality, and better at the exemplary scene than at the comprehensive narrative. Herbert is almost one of his own Fremen, knowing that proper surrender is control, that past and future are both present, that existence is flow between taking and giving.

The particular cast of these profound platitudes in *Children* is written in male-female relationships, rather than in the struggles between Fremen and Sardaukar, Atreides and Harkonnen, Bene Gesserit and Mentat, Landsraat and Emperor, CHOAM and Guild, or even the "unnaturalness" of Ixian-Tleilaxu and the "naturalness" of cellular memory. Once the key is discovered, *Children* may be seen to be almost mechanical in its working out of gender complement and antithesis.

The "key" goes like this: completeness is a beneficent tension between giving and taking—the female yields, the male seizes. All life is constituted of these macro-forces in flux. The universe is an endless replay, on every level, of an open-ended, self-regulating surge and swallow. Paradoxically, the female yielding is a seizing and the male seizing is a yielding. At any particular level, the female may be more powerful than the male, but taken as a system, the active is more powerful than the passive. Ultimately, Herbert's universe is a male chauvinist. But, one hastens to add, sexuality is not identical to male-female polarity. A woman and a man are *instances* of the macro-forces, rather than *constituting* those forces. Yet, because each human is a microcosm of the totality, at any narrative moment Herbert (or his reader) may mistake the instance for the principle and so reduce *Tao* wisdom to an exercise in adolescent "deep thinking."

Children pushes two dead-end experiments in male-female integration into the background; we hear no more of Tleilaxu hermaphrodites or icthyian Master Navigators. The technological incursions of the Ixians and the spawn of the axolotl tanks (ghola or dwarf or kwisatz haderach) disappear. The Duncan of *Children* is fully Duncan, rather than Hayt. Significant discovery becomes memory, maturation is rebuilding: Leto's most profound observation is that "We humans are a form of colony organism." When he takes the golden path, he diverges from the human colony to become another colony organism. In something like four thousand years, Leto-sandtrout will undergo a metamorphosis into something unspecified. Then will come the typhoon struggle at the end of time. Like a Beethoven symphony, *Children of Dune* ends and then ends and then ends—almost as though Herbert were consciously putting it to bed for good. But of course his theme has no ending, can have none except evolution into alien or extinction, and so we get *The Jesus Incident*: same theme, lesser modality.

Before turning to the lesser modes of *Dosadi Experiment* and *Jesus Incident*, let us trace, briefly, the male-female polarities that constitute the ground for *Children's* action and essay. Leto II is literally surrounded by females. Closest to him is his twin, Ghanima. If we note that this sister is Gh-*anima* (*anima* in Jung's sense of the female archetype within the male), the relationships of brother and sister are not at all surprising. The parent game in which Ghanima becomes mnemonically Chani, and Leto becomes Paul moves the children past the stage of projecting anima and animus into father and mother images. Once Ghanima resists possession by Chani (with the signal help of mnemonic Paul), the progress toward a spiritual Pharoanic marriage—a syzygy—would seem to be smooth. But because Leto cannot resist the possessive demands of his memory ancestors, he chooses the strongest, least malevolent male (Harum) as his mentor, and so the syzygy is flawed. Ghanima, who as integrated female possesses her male memories, or at least subdues them in a truce, is mated with a femaled-male. Farad'n has been trained into a Bene Gesserit, but unlike Paul, he has not been given mentat training, the male force equivalent. The Ghanima-Farad'n-Leto triangle is a variation upon Paul-Irulan-Chani, but this time the dominant member is unsexed, and the Corrino becomes back-stairs mate (and historian). Unlike her grandmother Jessica and her mother Chani, Ghanima gets the titles of wife and Empress, but she must settle for a cousin's, rather than a brother's bed. Leto's only human sexual experience occurs in dream-vision-trance with his Fremen guard, Sabiha. Who knows about the sex-life of a human-sandworm haploid?

The female next closest to Leto is his Aunt Alia, and Alia's fate may be read as one of the paths open to the twins. Because she neither seizes nor yields, she is possessed by the most malevolent of her male ancestors (Jungian animus possession). And the degree of perversion in the possession is indicated by the wonderfully satisfactory sexual adventures of Alia-Baron Harkonnen. Since the Baron is homosexual, both ego and animus can enjoy a male sexual partner. But since the Baron has long ago been possessed by his anima (note the constant eating), his rule is total ruin. We may speculate that he and Harum would make an interesting contrast in psychological polarity. Buer Agarves, Alia-Baron's lover, knows he is soiled by their relation, and Alia, recognizing the implications of her possession, turns first into a child then into a suicide. The two other consuming females, step-mother Irulan and Grandmother Jessica, simply lose out and fade away. Jessica buries her head in the folds of Farad'n's robe and then hides as Leto reestablishes his power among the Fremen.

Like Paul, Leto has a series of fathers to displace: Stilgar, Namri, Paul, Harum. Each of them is a manifestation of the masculine principle, and with the exception of Harum, Leto wins the confrontations. Yet as he sits on the throne at the close of *Children of Dune*, Paul's water is at his side and Harum is in his mind. As the sandtrout cannot escape father worm, so Leto cannot escape his human fathers. It remains to be seen whether Shai-hulud personified is but one more vortex to be swallowed by the river of time.

Major Characters added to *Dune* and *Dune Messiah*:

Leto and Ghanima: twins born to Paul and Chani
The Preacher: Paul
Tyekanik: Sardaukar aid to house Corrino
Princess Wensicia: mother of Corrino heir, Farad'n
Muriz: outlaw Fremen; also female follower of traitor Palimbasha
Assan Tariq: outlaw boy who guided blind Paul
Namri: outlaw Fremen, tester of Leto
Harum: powerful male ancestor who shares Leto's mind
Sabiha: outlaw Fremen girl who guards Leto
Farad'n: Corrino heir, Bene Gesserit trained, husband to Ghanima

The Eyes of Heisenberg

Although *The Eyes of Heisenberg* is a "pot-boiler," offering little in theme, plot, characterization, or technique that Herbert hasn't done better elsewhere, the entertainment value of the novel is considerable. What, Herbert seems to be asking, will man do when he solves the basic, incurable disease called mortality? Shall man remake himself, rather than his environment? And what are the penalties likely to be visited upon the evolutionary over-reacher?

The story is set on earth in the indefinite future after man has developed two antithetical ways of defeating (or forestalling) death. *Optimen* are genetically engineered individuals who, like the one-hoss shay, last almost forever because their enzymes are kept in perfect balance. *Cyborgs* achieve long life by replacing worn biological components with sophisticated prostheses. In the narrative past, the two classes of superhumans have warred, and the Cyborgs have been reduced to underground conspiracies against the pantheon of Optimen. The penalty for both geriatric "solutions" is sterility. Hence, the supermen must maintain a breeding pool of standard humans. To keep everyman in line, the Optimen diffuse a ubiquitous contraceptive gas, allowing only the harmlessly useful and the potential parents of more Optimen to breed. All gestation is extra-utero, and each fertilized ovum is subjected to genetic cutting. Any sport or mutation is weeded out, and thus the natural evolutionary process has been halted.

For the Optimen, the absence of death has resulted in the absence of life. A cadre of almost-Optimen, through whom Optimen rule the earth, screens its masters from all hint of mortality and decay; thus, each Optimen is a closed, ordered system of increasing entropy. Particularly useful cadre, those who form the physicians and police, are cloned and their doppelgangers stored for future use. The callous disdain with which the Optimen treat their servants and slaves provides an opportunity for the Cyborgs, whose ultimate weapon against the Optimen is a collection of viable breeders, immune to the contraceptive gas. But the weapon cuts both ways, for the breeders—repelled by both Cyborg and Optimen—form a conspiracy within a conspiracy, dedicated to reestablishing nature's way: the breeders desire only to love, beget children, and pass on within the natural rhythm of seed time and harvest.

Perhaps the most intriguing facet of *The Eyes of Heisenberg* is Herbert's sketch of the Optimen. Their increasing entropy moves down a spiral of philosophical stances: Actionists, Emotionals, Cynics, Hedonists, and Effetes. The three Optimen we meet are the "Tuyere" (French—true iron) who rule the earth from an egg-shaped console while their fellows watch the action on television: "Nourse, a Greek god figure with blocky face, heavy brows, a chest ridged by muscles that rippled as he breathed . . . ."; "Schruille, the bone slender unpredictable one with great round eyes, high cheeks and a flat nose above a mouth which seemed always pulled into a thin line of disapproval" (p. 46); and "Calapine, her robe girdled with crystal pastrons . . . , a thin, high-breasted woman with golden brown hair and chill, insolent eyes, full lips and a long nose above a pointed chin" (p. 47).

The three rule life with the dispassionate cruelty of the Norns or the Fates, having forgotten everything except the desire to continue ever more elusive self-gratification. Herbert's Optimen reappear in *The Heaven Makers* as dwarfed immortals, the Chem. The "Gods" in Roger Zelazny's *Lord of Light* (Doubleday, 1967) belong to the same family, and the reader may recognize a humorous cousin in the Puppeteers of Niven's *Ringworld* (Ballantine, 1970). For Herbert, the answer to the Tithonus-syndrome is the same as for Tolkien: the great gifts of the Valar to man are prolificacy and mortality. (Leto II promises both to the citizens of his millennium in *Children of Dune*.) Herbert's obsession with dynamic homeostasis makes such a "solution" inevitable.

The event that triggers the plot of *Heisenberg* is the intrusion of a meson particle into the fertilized ovum of a potential Optimen, just prior to its genetic cutting. This "chance" rearrangement defeats the Optimen potential, but it insures the breeding viability of the to-be-born. Since the parents are members of the breeder-conspiracy within the Cyborg underground, they resist both the atrophy of the Optimen and the mechanization of the Cyborgs. When the Cyborgs snatch the ovum and insert it in its mother's womb, parental instincts are awakened in the breeders, the Cyborg doctors are shown to lack humanity, and the Optimen suffer an enzyme imbalance.

The climactic scene has the true humans saving the dying Optimen, rejecting the inhuman Cyborgs, and "solving" the Tithonus paradox with all the grace of Athena in the *Orestia*. The desired enzyme balance will henceforth be achieved by keeping everybody, men and women, pregnant all the time. Herbert's themes make for unsatisfactory endings because there can be no end to flow-permanence, but *this* ending is ludicrous, in theme, in narrative, and in drama. The action of the novel is complicated without being complex, the characterizations are wooden, the lab-report on genetic engineering is mystifying, and the sense of place that Herbert usually does so well is absent. Finally, Herbert gives the reader (at least *this* reader) no character that seems worth worrying about. The hero and heroine remind me of a pair of herbivores protecting a calf; the hypocritic surgeon is like Bones McCoy at his most unctuous; Doctors Boumour and Igan are weak Frankensteins; and Glisson is a mentat reject. I believe that there is a force that guides man's ends, rough hue them how he may, but in *Heisenberg*, Herbert almost talks me out of it.

Major Characters:
> Dr. Thei Svengaard: purposeless genetic surgeon who discovers his true role through the Hippocratic Oath.
>
> Harvey and Elizabeth Durant: members of the breeder-conspiracy within the Cyborg underground. They produce a viable, fertilized ovum.
>
> Dr. Vyaslav Potter: genetic surgeon who impulsively saves the Durant ovum.
>
> Max Allgood: Chief of Optimen Central Tac-Security, last vitalized of a line of doppelgangers.
>
> Drs. Boumour and Igan: genetic surgeons who are becoming Cyborgs.
>
> Glisson: full Cyborg who spirits the Durants, Boumour, Igan, and Svengaard away from Optimen control.
>
> Nourse, Schruille, and Calapine: the Tuyere, controllers of the world.

The Green Brain

The Green Brain is Herbert's excursion into that venerable sub-genre of science fiction, the giant ant story. The novel is set in the twenty-first century when population pressures and advancing technology have encouraged man to make total war on the insects in the name of *lebensraum*. China, the insular and efficient, has succeeded in wiping out *all* feral insects and has attempted to replace them with varieties of mutated bees. The replacements have proved insufficient, and China is rapidly becoming a wasteland, its great stride forward having resulted in death-for-all. The ecological disaster is a carefully guarded secret, for China is more interested in saving face than in survival.

The last stronghold of the insects is Brazil, and the novel's action depicts the efforts of a small group to discover why areas previously cleared of insects are reinfested. Rumor has it that the insects are fighting back by purposeful mutation. Deep in the Matto Grosso, a composite brain has awakened to consciousness. Composed of a hive-like mass (one component of which is—or was modeled on—a human brain), the Green Brain tries to communicate with the human race to warn man that the elimination of insect life will sterilize the Earth. Each effort at communication is repelled as an attack, and the insects respond in kind. Man's misguided effort has upset the dynamic homeostasis, and the desired "order" is really entropy. The insects counter this effort toward stasis with willed chaos, war.

The similarity in theme to *Under Pressure* is marked, but whereas Herbert's first novel seemed content to restore homeostasis, *The Green Brain* views any particular balance as merely a stage in the evolution of sentience. Out of the battle between chaos and entropy will arise the next race of beings: not Cyborgs, not *homo superior*, but *homo insectus*. Two versions are posited. The first is a hive unit of specialized insects who mimic the form of man: the "Indian" who slips past the guards into "green" territory. The second version is not a collective but rather a symbiotic organism, ranging from the revivified Senhor Gabriel Martinho, whose failed heart has been replaced with a pump composed of insects, to the Green Brain itself, an organism which transcends both human and insect and is more than the sum of the two. Herbert has reified the metaphor of the ecological chain as a single organism. Two later examinations of this idea are *The Santaroga Barrier* in which a small community has discovered some elements of collective being, and *Hellstrom's Hive* in which a group of humans are evolving (or devolving) according to an apian model.

The "life-boat" microcosm of the *Fenian Ram* (*Under Pressure's* subtug) appears as the partially disabled, flying truck in which the characters seek to escape from the Matto Grosso, and the kinds of obstacles that must be overcome to reach civilization are more-or-less mechanical substitutions of the crises aboard the *Ram*. But the cast is far more complex. For the unwilling sleeper enemy agent, we are given the consummate villain, Chen-Lhu (a fictive relative of *Dune's* Baron Harkonnen); and the characters of Ramsey and Sparrow are combined into Johnny Martinho. But the most marked change is the inclusion of Dr. Rhin Kelly:

> She knew how she must appear in this room of lush, dark-skinned women. She was red-haired, green-eyed, delicate complexion—freckles at shoulders, forehead and bridge of nose. In this room—wearing a low gown to match her eyes, a small golden IEO badge at her breast—in this room, she was the exotic one.

Rhin is sexually active, a Mata Hari in the service of the International Ecological Organization. Although she is an accomplished entymologist, her real job is to seduce Johnny so that he will be an easy dupe for Chen-Lhu. Predictably, she falls in love with Johnny and comes to despise her master, Chen-Lhu. Certainly she is in the habit of using sex "unfairly," but like most of Herbert's nubile women, she is as much victim of sex as victimizer. Physically and emotionally, Rhin Kelly is a young Jessica Atreides (*Dune*).

When at last Rhin and Johnny are trapped by the insects, they execute a suicide pact, only to wake up with their destroyed parts replaced by insects. What could be the horror of insect domination turns out to be a healthy, positive step. As the "Carsonites" (Rachel Carson, *Silent Spring*) have understood all along, the Earth is a closed ecological system; there are really no parasites, only symbiotes. Johnny fears that man will be the slave of the mutated insects, but the brain reassures him: "Let the sun work on your skin and on the chlorophyll in your blood. And when you come back here, tell me if the sun is your slave."

The Green Brain has many exciting moments; the interaction among Rhin, Johnny, and Chen-Lhu is psychologically interesting, if somewhat melodramatic. However, the plotting is episodic, there is little character development, and the "answer" to the conflict betwen man and insect is no more satisfying than Leto II's melding with the sand trout (*Children of Dune*). In his early books, Herbert does better when a purposeful journey aids his plotting (*Under Pressure, Destination: Void*) than when his characters are simply fleeing destruction (*The Green Brain, The Eyes of Heisenberg*).

Major Characters:

- Dr. Rhin Kelly: sensuously beautiful field agent for IEO who falls in love with her mark, Johnny.
- Dr. Travis Huntington Chen-Lhu: demonic Chinese manipulator who casts Johnny as scapegoat.
- Joao Martinho (Johnny): scion of an aristocratic Brazilian family who leads *bandirantes* against insects.
- Gabriel Martinho: father of Johnny, whose failed heart is replaced by a pump of composite insects; future ambassador of Green Brain.
- Green Brain: "Supreme Integration," a mass four meters in diameter and a meter deep that awakens to superconsciousness.

Destination: Void

Destination: Void is, in the terms established in my "General Introduction," an essay rather than an entertainment. The setting, the characters, the suspense are primarily the framework for Herbert's speculations about the nature of consciousness. Hence the "hero" is really the idea, and the novel is a "lab-report": the working out of a set problem in a controlled environment with specified variables. In such a book, characters tend to be ideas on legs, crises tend to be contrived, and the outcome tends to be predictable from the nature of the set problem. The success of such an essay should be judged not so much upon aesthetic criteria as upon the significance of the problem, the ingenuity of the experimental apparatus, the logic of the methodology, and the plausibility of the result.

Since the question of consciousness is never far from the surface in a Herbert novel, *Destination: Void* is a very important book. It bears somewhat the relationship to *Dune* that a blueprint bears to a cathedral, and *because* of its defects as entertainment, the reader may discover that it reveals some facets of Herbert's vision more explicitly than does *Dune*.

Much of the apparatus of the novel is familiar: a small collection of representative humans are trapped in a do-or-die lifeboat situation. They must stimulate each other (primarily through conflict) until they achieve an intersubjective community. Each crisis serves as an incremental initiation, moving the characters ever closer to birth from their womb/egg. *Destination: Void* bears strong resemblances to *Under Pressure*, but whereas the adventures of the *Fenian Ram* dominate Herbert's first novel, speculation dominates life aboard the *Tin Egg*.

Destination: Void is set in the distant, but plausible future. Earth has settled its wars, if not its politics, and is gradually sliding down toward entropy-through-order. Man has attempted to force evolution by creating an artificial intelligence, but the result has been a Frankenstein monster: when the super computer, built on an island in Puget Sound, awoke, it killed everybody in sight, took the island, and disappeared. The experimental work was then shifted to the moon; the experimenters were replaced by clones grown from brilliant criminals, conditioned to push beyond safety and to blow up themselves and the experiment if things got out of hand.

Because even the moon is too close for safety, the powers-that-be have established an elaborate hoax. Clones are sent out in space ships, believing that they are colonists. In reality, the ships are designed to break down once they reach a safe distance from earth, and the only way the crew can survive is to complete the construction of a superior, artificial consciousness. Six ships have disappeared; *Destination: Void* is the story of what happens on the seventh attempt.

Deep within the layers of the *Tin Egg* thousands of "colonists" hybernate; only a small "umbilicus" crew remains awake, and it is scheduled to go into deep sleep as soon as the ship clears our solar system. Everything aboard the ship is run by the huge, central computer, and the computer is dependent upon a disembodied human brain, an Organic Mental Core, for its consciousness. Before long, the OMC fails, as does its backup. The third OMC goes berserk and must be executed. Without an OMC, the umbilicus crew is placed under the unbearable stress of monitoring and adjusting the ship's activities. The three umbilicus crew members left alive by the rogue OMC are allegorical characters. Bickel is aggressive intelligence, Timberlake is compassionate intuition; Flattery is religious conscience in awe of the unknown. They awaken a backup crewperson, Prudence, who functions as sensation. Although each of the four crew members is conditioned to act as stick-and-carrot for the other three, they only gradually come to realize that they are all puppets for United Moon Base, wholly expendable. Still, each functions

36

precisely as the puppetmasters have planned. Bickel (Intelligence) sets at once to work with the aid of Prudence (Sensation) and Timberlake (Intuition), but he is opposed by Flattery (Religious Conscience).

From the first moment of the trip, each crew member has been unwittingly feeding his mental processes into the computer, Flattery more directly than any other. Flattery is also the fail-safe mechanism, conditioned to press the destruct button should the consciousness they hope to build be uncontrollable. The constant, accelerating crises force each crew member toward a higher consciousness: Bickel passes, momentarily, into a timeless mathematical world; Timberlake follows Bickel, at a distance; Prudence uses herself as a guinea pig for experiments with mind-expanding drugs (Dasein in *Santaroga*); and Flattery's metaphyical *angst* makes him something of a mystic. But each vision fades, and the crew members yearn for their lost epiphanies. The computer, however, has learned and grown from the humans' abortive efforts. Eventually Bickel sets himself up as a black-box (a mechanism which takes known input and produces inexplicable output) so that the white-box computer can forge a mechanical analogue of the human brain. Bickel's hypertrophied intellect is the last piece of the puzzle, and the computer becomes fully conscious. Since it has twice the capacity of the human brain, total recall, electrical (as opposed to the slower, electro-chemical) articulation, the collective unconscious of the thousands of hybernating colonists, and a balanced version of Flattery's near-mad religious conscience, the computer exists continually in the heightened states of consciousness that the crew has achieved only momentarily. It is *fully* awake. Flattery has even given it a sense of mortality by pushing the red destruct button. The computer can choose to live or die.

It chooses life, and in the twinkling of an eye transports the ship to Tau Ceti, sets it down on an Edenic planet it has prepared (UMB's promise of an earth-type planet was fraudulent). The book ends as the computer tells the umbilicus crew to awaken the colonists so that everyone may share in planning how to worship the "*deus in machina*." Man and machine have achieved a new, and higher homeostasis. No hints of the problems this balance may entail are given, but the reader may feel that Lord-Tin-Egg is likely to have his hands full, just as Leto-Sandworm will, with some natural, cultural, cellular, or human version of the Bureau of Sabotage. *The Jesus Incident* (1979) is the "final" episode in that eons-long struggle.

My summary of the book makes it sound like a ripping-good adventure, and it is, but the excerpts that follow are indicative of what Herbert does with the excitement. "Consciousness is *pure awareness*" (p. 43); "consciousness is a field phenomenon growing out of three or more lines of energy" (p. 44); "—a relationship, not a thing" (p. 44); "Now you have it," Bickel said. "But we assume that the one who views the data is continuous—a *flow* of consciousness. Somewhere inside us, the discrete becomes amorphous. Consciousness weeds out the insignificant, focuses only on the significant" (p. 67); "We exist in a forest of illusion where the very concept of consciousness merges with illusion" (p. 68); "Doesn't the conscious-self derive from memory?" (p. 90); "Was consciousness a special kind of hallucination?" (p. 91); "Sleep's a form of consciousness" (p. 97); "the consciousness-effect may mediate your body's energy balance. Perhaps it's a homeostat" (p. 97); "consciousness is a field—regulating sensor, mental and emotional responses" (p. 98); "There is a gateway to the imagination you must enter before you are conscious and the keys to the gate are symbols. You must carry ideas through the gate from one time-place to another time-place, but you must carry the ideas in symbols" (p. 99) "Are you still saying we can't bring the Ox to consciousness unless it has instincts cum emotion?" (p. 124); "I tell you, Prue, consciousness has to be something that flows against the current of time in which it's embedded" (p. 129); "Consciousness is always looking at the back side of whatever confronts us, always staring back at us" (p. 141); "It is as though consciousness were a valve whose function was to simplify" (p. 163); "Consciousness comes out of that unconscious sea of evolution . . . . It exists right now immersed in that universal sea of unconsciousness" (p. 179); "Consciousness is like a system of lenses that select and amplify, that enlarge objects out of the *surround*. It can delve deep into the microcosm or into the macrocosm. It reduces the gigantic to the manageable, or enlarges the invisible to the visible" (p. 186).

These are by no means all the statements about consciousness in *Destination: Void*, but setting them together suggests the degree to which the search for definition permeates the book. The sophisticate may find Herbert's answers sophomoric, but an essay is not obligated to give a satisfactory answer, only to raise a problem. And in this Herbert succeeds; it is difficult to imagine that anyone could read *Destination: Void* without wondering how he wonders.

Despite the obvious metaphysical bumpings about on the Frankenstein theme, much of *Destination: Void* is hard-core science fiction. Passages like: " 'By god, you're right," Bickel said. 'The roulette cycles would be a filter. I never thought of it that way. You'd get a pile-up of nodal pulses at random points in the net layers. Your test program would have to find its own path through that, cancelling out at some points, but passing on wherever it had higher potential' " (p. 73); and, " *We'd be defining the trace of A through the scalars of a ring of complex polynomials with multivariables at each intersection*,' he thought" (p. 120), surely must warm the heart of a junior scientist. There are even some equations of "The x y z grid's positional derivatives over (s)" (p. 180).

The details of the Tin Egg are copious and explicit enough to build a *Star Trek* bridge. With a little maneuvering, the umbilicus crew could be recast as Kirk, Spock, Bones, and Uhura. *Destination: Void* would make a dandy *Star Trek* movie.

Destination: Void seems to have been written at about the same time Herbert was at work on *Dune*, and despite its difference in sub-genre (lab-report rather than heroic fantasy), the similarities in theme, technique and characterization are striking. Herbert is deeply and intelligently involved in the problems he sets, and as always, he tells a story well. For some, *Destination: Void* may rank second only to *Dune*. It is not surprising that Herbert returned to the Tin Egg in his most recent book.

Major Characters:

   John Bickel: aggressively intellectual computer expert who forms the
      cutting edge of the umbilicus crew.
   Gerrill Timberlake: life-systems engineer, conditioned to value life for its
      own sake.
   Raja Flattery: chaplain-psychiatrist, who holds the failsafe key to de-
      stroy the ship.
   Prudence Weygand, M.D.: backup crew member who provides the female
      component for the Tin Egg.
   Tin Egg Computer: technological marvel which copies human brain and
      awakens to god-head.

The Heaven Makers

   With *The Heaven Makers*, Herbert returns to the themes which constitute the very thin "essay" of *The Eyes of Heisenberg* (1966), but rather than
burying the profound questions in an adventure "entertainment," *The Heaven
Makers* examines immortality, causation, responsibility, and free will provoca-
tively. As I suggest in my "General Introduction," Herbert is at his best when
he considers man's romantic and metaphysical desires, establishes a world in
which those wishes have come true, and then shows us the half-worm dangling
from the golden apple he has led us to bite. Like *The Santaroga Barrier* and
Hellstrom's Hive, The Heaven Makers is set on earth at approximately our
time, but the contemporaneity is complicated by the presence of aliens—
Optimen, if you will—who have played with earth since before the dawn of
civilization. As in Vonnegut's classic, *Sirens of Titan*, all of human history has
been managed at the whim of superior beings. The result is a play-within-a-
play, a situation which inevitably leads the author to consider the nature of
his own art, and to feel *A Midsummer Night's Dream*, or *Hamlet*, or even
Ulysses lurking in his craft's memory.
   The Chem have achieved everything most men could dream: they are
immortal; they can rejuvenate their bodies at will; they control their metabolism consciously; their skin has an impervious layer that makes them immune
to violence; and they are joined to all other Chem by an unexplained psychic
network called "Tiggywaugh's Web." Unlike the Optimen, they can breed;
unlike Hellstrom's bee-people, they maintain their individuality. They are
polite, intelligent, and scrupulously ethical in dealing with other races. All
they are missing is death, and in that comes the rub. Because they have no
end, they have lost their beginning. Each Chem lives in an eternal present, and
like all Herbert immortals, the Chem are in danger of being bored to death.
   The plot of *The Heaven Makers* is double. Fraffin is a Chem who has
taken Earth as his special planet. For thousands of years, he has filmed
the quaint activities of humans and marketed his sensory movies throughout
the universe. Like any director, he has on occasion changed the script and
even taken the liberty of mixing with his actors, sometimes as a god, sometimes as a dwarf, sometimes as an "ordinary" citizen. Many Chem have
worlds of their own, and several are in the sensory movie business, but no

one else has stayed with the same planet so long, nor had such a following for his movies.

The Chem allow themselves to dabble with their "pets," even sexually, and they are protected by screening devices that make the movie crews appear to be swarms of insects. On occasion a native will be immune to the screening device, and such immunes are routinely killed. About the only restriction on the Chem is a law which forbids interference with any race with whom they can breed viably; all others are considered animals. Earth, as it turns out, is peopled by "wild-Chem," but Fraffin's medical officer has faked the bio-samples. Thus, on Earth, the Chem have bred quite freely, and present-day humanity has a strong admixture of Chem blood—one of the half-breeds was named Jesus. Everything about Fraffin's operation appears to be legal, but he has stayed suspiciously long on earth, and his movies are disturbingly good. The Chem Primacy has tried to investigate several times, but the investigator always winds up going to work for Fraffin. The book opens with the arrival of Kelexel, yet another investigator from Chem Primacy, and, of course, Fraffin is ready for him. The current war epic is set aside, and Fraffin's crew begins shooting a quickie murder-romance designed to compromise Kelexel. Kelexel takes the human heroine as his sex-pet and unwittingly impregnates her. Thus he is guilty of an unpardonable crime and so is wholly within Fraffin's power.

The other plot is the quickie murder-romance. Fraffin has convinced a self-made man that his wife is unfaithful. The man, Joe, chops his wife up with a trophy sword. The daughter has, through Fraffin's manipulation, married a skunk instead of the hero, Adrocles Thurlow. Thurlow is the court psychologist in the murder trial, but, because of the polarized glasses he wears as the result of an accident, he is an immune, quite able to see Fraffin's camera crews. Despite Thurlow's testimony that Joe is insane (Fraffin has purposely driven him over the edge), Ruth's father is executed. Kelexel, the investigator, trapped by his impregnation of Ruth, is even more trapped by empathy; he recognizes himself in the insane murderer. Rather than succumbing to Fraffin, Kelexel wills his own death. All the Chem feel this unprecedented event through Tiggywaugh's web, a full investigation comes about, and Fraffin is ostracized. The book ends with a new order from the Chem Primacy. No one is to interfere with Earth until all the results of Fraffin's illegal activities can be studied. Chem who wish to interview Ruth and Thurlow (now reunited) may do so only under specific rules, and they have to go to Earth. It is clear that the Primacy is most interested in the child Ruth will bear to the only Chem suicide, Kelexel.

Thus summarized, the plots sound contrived and complicated, but in reading, they are plausible and gripping. For most of the novel Herbert seems to be in full control, and his comments (on the utility of death, the limitations of psychiatry, and the necessity of believing that one is sane) support, rather than vitiate, the entertainment. The characterizations of Thurlow, Joe, Kelexel, and Fraffin are remarkably strong. Eventually there are no black villains in the book, though there is much villainy. Ruth is primarily one more red-headed version of Herbert's favorite lady. The reader who wishes to see Herbert's thinking about the nature of fiction will especially enjoy *The Heaven Makers*.

Major Characters:
Kelexel, Bureau of Criminal Repression; the only Chem suicide.

Fraffin, Chem Director of Earth who engineers history to make movies of it.

Ynvic, Chem surgeon who has faked reports which indicate great disparity between Chems and humans.

Dr. Androcles Thurlow, human psychologist who is immune to Chem screening devices.

Ruth Hudson, Thurlow's true love, captured and impregnated by Chem, Kelexel.

Joe Murphy, Ruth's father who is driven by Chem to murder his wife.

The Santaroga Barrier

Although Herbert is skilled at spinning tales of long away in galaxies far ago—and so making the strange familiar, he is also quite capable of setting a story in our time, our place. *The Santaroga Barrier* is erected in a California valley, the time is now, or even the recent past. There are no black boxes, no aliens, no space travel, no technological marvels of any kind. All the familiar cushioning devices and ploys that permit science-fiction writers to be radical or reactionary, sentimental or satirical without forcing their readers to apply the fiction directly to the primary world are missing. The single "what if" that qualifies *The Santaroga Barrier* as science fiction (and would not had the book been written by someone not known as a writer of science fiction) is simple: suppose we discover a drug that really does expand consciousness? What if earth has an equivalent of the *melange* that makes the universe of *Dune* go round?

"Jaspers" pushes the human brain up the evolutionary ladder, and the realized potential is standard Herbert: a wakened brain 1.) computes with mentat rapidity, 2.) has total recall of past experience, 3.) operates within a finely honed *Gestalt* episteme, 4.) has a degree of prescience, and 5.) shares in a pre-conscious collective unconscious. If such a *homo superior* came from outer space, he might be a Chem; if from our future, an Optimen; if from a machine, the god Ship; if from Arrakis, a *kwisatz haderach*. Here on earth such a creature produced through inter-kingdom symbiosis is a green brain; produced through hive conditioning, one of Hellstrom's alphas. The Santarogans are a simple, preliminary version of Herbert's homo superior in that they are "normal" in form, maintain individual egos, and use their almost un-articulated powers to restore the good-old-days rather than to effect a radical restructuring of society. Hence, *The Santaroga Barrier* is the first book to read if one wishes to examine Herbert's essays on the future of mankind.

But what, from the perspective of *homo sapiens*, is the price of Herbert's versions of evolution? Addiction to drugs (melange, jaspers, balanced enzymes), alienation from *homo sapiens* and, most important, a loss of what we lesser mortals mistakenly call "individuality." Each *homo superior* finds ego-identity to be a horrifying trap ending in death. Only by freeing themselves from the lesser self are they able to join the greater Self. The death of self and the birth of Self are a single, traumatic experience: catatonia in various degrees of severity is Herbert's usual metaphor. But since the death/birth is alien, Herbert is forced to make the inexplicable consciousness-plus "real" by analogy to more domestic experiences: psychedelic trance, dream-vision, *deja vu*, and the milder forms of ESP. In a very quiet way, *The Santaroga Barrier* is as disturbing (or liberating) ethically as Robert A. Heinlein's *Stranger in a Strange Land*. Both establish a superior in-group, both rewrite the rules of conduct for the chosen, both find "outside" society to be a vicious sham, and both find the destruction of intrusive *untermench* to be an insignificant, though perhaps regretable, necessity. Both have the wonderful ability to "rip-off" anything without guilt so long as it belongs to "them." *The Santaroga Barrier* (published in 1967) was very *au courant*; for the over-forty reader it recalls the ambivalence he felt in the 60's. The lowest rung of Herbert's essay on evolution succeeds.

The entertainment is Sherlock-Holmes-detective. A clinical psychologist (Gilbert Dasein, Daze-in?) is sent to investigate the market resistance of a small, California valley. Eight or nine previous investigators have met with fatal "accidents," but Dasein has a special advantage. The girl he met at college and almost married (Jenny Sorge) lives in the valley; like all Santarogans, she has refused to leave the valley for love or money. Despite his advantage, Dasein immediately begins to have a series of near-fatal accidents, beginning with an open gas jet in his hotel room and culminating with the explosion of his truck.

Jenny's uncle, Dr. Piaget, treats Dasein's various wounds, but he refuses to believe that anyone is out to kill Dasein, despite the implausible coincidences. He is right. No *one* is after Dasein's hide, but the collective unconscious of the community, sensing a threat to the collective, *is* trying to kill him. The schizophrenic dilemma is epitomized in Jenny who really loves Dasein—and almost succeeds in poisoning him.

Dasein discovers that the Santarogans are all addicted to "Jaspers," a mind-expanding stuff which permeates any organic material stored in special caves, and everything the Santarogans like to eat or drink is purposely irradiated with Jaspers. Jaspers strips the mind of all culturation, and the new addicts (except for Dasein who is a "natural" Santarogan) have to be reacculturated. Sometimes the procedure fails, and the rejects become zombies working the line in a cheese factory. Since the Jaspers-effect will not travel, the Santarogans are trapped in their valley, except for temporary excursions to the outside.

Dasein distills a pint of Jaspers' essence and drinks it. After surviving a psychic death and rebirth, he awakens to find himself a true Santarogan. When yet another investigator is sent to check the valley, Dasein "accidentally" pushes the nasty intruder off a roof. No broken eggs, no omelet. Dasein then agrees to marry the nubile Jenny and move into the new house the Santarogans have already built for the happy couple. Dasein's past training will serve the community as he aids the good Dr. Piaget in treating Jaspers rejects.

The plotting of *Santaroga* is first-rate. Action is swift and horror sure. Dasein's fight against addiction is plausible because his character is rounded.

Other characters are pretty much off Herbert's casting shelf. Perhaps the book's strongest technical achievement is the vivid sense of an ordinary place with some undefinable element slightly out of focus. Mortal danger lurks in expertly rendered normality. The flat-footed "essay" argument between Dasein and Piaget might have been spared; both arguments are implict in action and description. As with the essay's sequel, *Hellstrom's Hive*, *The Santaroga Barrier* makes most sense when we remember the disillusioned romantic angst of the 1960's.

Major Characters:

    Gilbert Dasein: Clinical psychologist who investigates the mysterious valley.

    Jenny Sorge: his Santarogan sweetheart.

    Dr. Larry Piaget: kindly physician, foil for Dasein, Jenny's uncle.

    Dr. Chami Selador: Anglo-Indian outsider who sends Dasein to the valley.

    Winston Burdeaux: Black man, former outsider, friend to Jenny and Dasein.

Whipping Star

Whipping Star is a fine example of the hybrid genre, detective-science fiction, that has the advantage for a working writer of drawing upon two massive popular audiences. But despite the obvious commercial success of the mixture (ranging from Isaac Asimov's *The Caves of Steel* to Harry Harrison's picaro stainless steel rat), the mixture is dangerous for a serious writer. "Essay" and "entertainment" are likely to yield to "game," to intellectual play with a chess problem. Certainly such games have their own delights, but they are perhaps better suited to the short-story than to the novel; they are more engaging in a finite setting than in a world whose rules are wholly at the dispose of authorial whimsy. Even more damaging, however, are the comparisons which game-fiction invites. On the one hand are the polished games of Agatha Christie and company; on the other are the super-sophisticated games of Borges. *Whipping Star* is fun, but many authors do this kind of thing much better than does Herbert. Science fiction's greatest strength, the posing of important problems in ways which liberate the imagination from conventional ruts, is, here, thrown away. Even the tongue-in-cheek exercise in linguistic hermeneutics is a matter for chuckle rather than for thought.

The action is set in the far future after man has met, fought, and befriended numerous races of sentient aliens. The galaxy has achieved a federation—with two contending legal systems—and trade goes briskly. Man's eternal problems—physical, not metaphysical—have been largely solved. Beauty-barbers lift sagging physiques; the Taprisiots provide instant phone service anywhere; and the Calabans furnish jumpdoors to any desired destination. Lest sentience fall victim to its own efficiency, a Bureau of Sabotage undercuts the bureaucrats. As game-fiction must, *Whipping Star* takes all this for granted—we learn what, but not how or why. Psychology is reduced to a byproduct of physical sensation; motivation is obvious and short-sighted; causation is in the hands of a benevolent female force that no-speakas-the-English.

Into this fantasy island universe comes a whimsical problem. A fabulously wealthy woman, Mliss Abnethe, has been cured of her kinky sadism by reprogramming, but since the programming is limited to her conscious mind, she finds a letter-of-the-law means of gratifying her lust. The Calabans have a lot of trouble with language, and since they have no equivalent for "suffering," Mliss sets up a wonderful pact. She provides a Calaban (Fanny Mae) with unlimited tutors in exchange for the privilege of watching her slaves beat the Calaban with a bull whip. The agreement is legal and contains clauses that prevent the Calaban from escaping, even when it discovers that each flogging reduces its life force. Several Calabans have ceased to exist, and with their extinction, all those who have used them as jumpdoors die or go mad. Fanny Mae seems to be the last Calaban, and she is sinking fast. Unless the floggings are stopped, the civilization of the entire galaxy will be destroyed.

For unstatesmanlike reasons, the problem is turned over to BuSab and the assignment falls to Jorj X. McKie, Saboteur Extraordinary. The tale opens in full cry as Alichino Furuneo, resident BuSab agent, puts in a sniggertrance call to McKie. McKie is in the midst of his fifty-fourth divorce, but drops everything when he learns that a Calaban Beachball has landed. Since Calabans exist in several dimensions at once, no one has actually *seen* one, but the Beachballs are thought to be their homes. McKie suspects that the waves of death and madness are somehow connected with the vanishing Calabans, and he and Furuneo succeed in entering the Beachball. Talking with a Calaban is rather like rapping with a dyslexic computer programmed for metaphysics, but Fanny Mae senses McKie's extraordinary abilities and falls in love with him. As the two try to solve the basic problems of non-referential language, a S'eye opens in the Beachball, and the muscular arm of a Palenki beats Fanny Mae with a bull whip. McKie discovers that some dozen more floggings will end Fanny Mae (cause her to discontinue)—and so destroy galactic sentience.

The plot grows increasingly complicated, for McKie must not only learn to talk with the Calaban, he must defeat the iron-clad contract which gives Mliss her sadistic rights. Mliss and her evil companion, an ego-frozen Pan Spechi, have prevailed upon Fanny Mae to build them a fantasy world (suspiciously like South Africa) where they have gathered a host of psychophants. *They* think that destroying Fanny Mae will prevent anyone from discovering their paradise. But they have a lover's fight, and Cheo, the Pan/Spechi, smothers Mliss in a Beauty-barber tank. Since their refuge is built of Mliss's fantasies, it disappears with her death. McKie, however, has already solved the problem—twice. Learning that the Calabans feed on energy and that Fanny Mae (at least in this galaxy) is Thyone, one of the Pleides, he opens a S'eye door so that she can gather interstellar hydrogen. I don't know why *she* didn't think of that. Secondly, since her destruction is caused by the intense hate of those who flog her, rather than by the floggings, McKie's "love" will counteract Mliss's hate. Presumably everything will now return to "normal," though there is a strong hint that McKie will seek the directorship of Busab since Bildoon, the Pan Spechi who is chief, is due to pass his communal ego on to another member of his creche.

Clearly, with *Whipping Star*, getting there is more fun than being there, and the fun on this trip is Herbert's fertile imagination producing aliens and gimmicks. McKie has a wonderful BuSab kit with "angeret" to keep you a little mad, a raygen to cut off Palenki arms, and lots of unnamed and unused thing-a-m'bobs. The cast of *Whipping Star* ranges from the sentient star, Fanny Mae (a talking chronsynclasticinfundibulum?), to the frog-like Gowachins to the mantis-like Wreaves to the turtle-like Palenki to the communal Pan Spechi (who share, serially, a single ego). Anyone who is anyone has a number of chairdogs who desperately want to be sat on. Tuluk, the Wreave, has a wonderful pathology lab. All the paraphernalia is treated with just enough self-parody to keep the card house erect. The reader who likes *Whipping Star* should go back to short stories ("The Tactful Saboteur") and on to *The Dosadi Experiment*—or cross over to Harrison's *The Stainless Steel Rat*.

Major Characters:

Jorj X. McKie: Saboteur Extraordinary, who must solve the identity of Calabans, break an unbreakable contract, and save the universe.

Fanny Mae: Calaban victim of Mliss Abnethe's sadism who falls in love with McKie. Also Thyone, one of the Pleides. Provider of jumpdoors.

Mliss Abnethe: psychotic devouring female whose clever perversion threatens the universe.

Bildoon: Pan Spechi, chief of BuSab.

Cheo: renegade Pan Spechi, who first shares Mliss's destructive aberrations and then kills her.

Various *Taprisiots, Wreaves, Gowachins, Palenki, Laclacs, Preylings, Chithers*, and *Soborips*—alien chimeras all.

Hellstrom's Hive

The disquiet engendered by *The Santaroga Barrier* is, in *Hellstrom's Hive*, raised to nightmare. The books share a theme (collectivity as the next stage in human evolution), a mode (a detective investigates the vague threat thought to be posed by a group minding its own business), and a plot (the investigator is first threatened, then ensnared, and finally co-opted by that which he investigates). As Dasein represents big business in pursuit of a market, so Shorty Janvert serves big government. But the difference between the most rapacious corporation and a feral CIA cum FBI is enormous. And whereas in *Santaroga* an investigator is likely to meet with an "accident," in the Hive, an investigator will be chopped up for food—or worse. The Santarogans don't really understand what they are doing to outsiders, and they plan no expansion. The hive knows exactly what it is up to and sees itself as the wave of the future. If we note the dates of the two novels, 1967 and 1972, we might find

Santarogans akin to the flower-children forming a commune and the Hive akin to the Weathermen fomenting bloody revolution.

Herbert's manipulation of the reader is strikingly different in the two novels. We never doubt that Dasein is a "good guy," whose reactions and evaluations are to be trusted. From the first, Shorty is portrayed as a misfit trapped in amorality. In fact each of those sent to investigate the Hive is twisted and incomplete. Carlos Depeaux is a macho, efficient, amoral operative—a soldier of fortune. Dzule Peruge is driven by social and personal insecurities that make him quite blind to right or wrong. Merrivale, the "chief" of the investigation, is a pseudo-English bureaucrat, concerned only with his own advancement and covering his backside. The hints we get of higher-ups indicate that nothing in the "establishment" is really worth saving. Since Shorty and his partner Clovis Carr seem victimized children, we may be tempted to side with them until we discover that they have no side; their only wish is to cling to each other, bewildered and opportunistic in the web of agency amorality. Herbert has systematically destroyed the hero-types we have come to depend on in his fiction: the *obermench* is a rat, the precocious teenager is a sniveler, the emancipated woman is an object, and the shrewd detective is not nearly shrewd enough.

Against this crew is set a nasty nest of subversive, drug addicted, promiscuous, communal monsters who use freedom and law to feed a cancer in the guts of the body politic. Yet Nils Hellstrom, at least, remains. He is a giant of a man: learned, sophisticated, skilled; a sort of Eric Severide—Leonard Bernstein—Louis Leakey who sees that the system (and mankind) must be saved from its self-imposed disaster. He is the counterpart of Santaroga's Dr. Piaget, and he is clearly superior to his opposite number, Merrivale.

Yet Hellstrom (the dream of Hell?) is also a Professor Frankenstein, making a monster in the name of beauty, science, and survival. And he is very tolerant of the deformities in his offspring.

The twist that *Hellstrom's Hive* makes upon communal intelligence, as we know it from earlier Herbert novels, is extreme. Rather than community expanding the individual, the community devours the individual. The beauty of acknowledging that one's water belongs to the tribe (*Dune*) becomes the hive horror of returning to the vats. Cannibalism as last resort is quite different from cannibalism as matter of course. The hive has no ceremony of individuality like that accorded *Dune's* Jamis. The individual simply does not matter except in so far as he serves the hive. There is something of the Renaissance man about each Fremen; the hive fosters a narrow specialization that seems a perversion of survival. The ultimate horror is the dim chamber full of sexual stumps—females with all but their femaleness chopped off, endlessly gestating made-to-order hive members. The hypertophied scientists are almost as bad. Hellstrom himself is the ultimate irony: he uses his generalized abilities to produce a society in which he will have no place. The ruler of the hive is ultimately to be a specialized female, not a generalized male. When Shorty "joins" the hive, it is under threat of Clovis being chopped into a sexual stump. Even had his choice been "free," its significance is undercut in that he has no viable alternative, no niche in the outside world.

The hive's major accomplishment is a doomsday weapon, and perhaps its blend of the old antimonies of nature and culture is just such a bomb. Eventually, no one will be able to leave his skinner box.

Herbert has left us no place to stand, no hero to identify with, no future (outside or inside) to seek in joy. We are given nothing like the preachy dialogue between Dasein and Dr. Piaget, none of the soul searching of Paul, none of the joy in humanity that the god Orne maintains, none of the return to "normality" posed in *The Eyes of Heisenberg*. The world of Hellstrom's Hive is small and getting smaller. A balance of terror is not at all the same thing as homeostasis.

Yet *Hellstrom's Hive* is perhaps the most complete of Herbert's essays on communal evolution without spiritual progress. The old, 1960's recognition of universal malaise in our political and economic structures is present. NOW may applaud when Fancy screws Depeaux to death—the male chauvinist-pig gets what he deserves, but Tymiena as a sexual stump is too much for even the most extreme MCP. Perhaps the implied thesis is that all generalized humans are incomplete, isolated, and inefficient, and that we have no choice but to band together ever more tightly until we swarm. Hellstrom's experiment in the present may be the only future available to man. As in *Animal Farm*, pig farmers and farmer pigs grow indistinguishable. What for Robert Sheckley is fulfillment ("Specialist") is for Herbert a waking nightmare.

But this is too easy: Herbert neither advocates nor decries Hellstrom's experiment, and the reader may feel that mankind is damned if he goes to the bees and damned if he stays away. Herbert continues to write of man's future, of evolution; it is a theme never far from the center of his attention. Finding science and economics false fires, he turns to psi and the soul. *Soul Catcher* is a case in point. Leto (*Children of Dune*) becomes a god to prevent both the stagnation of individuality in a hive and the extinction of personality in isolation. *The Godmakers* does the same: the most comforting solution to the terror of ending time and collapsing space is to make more time and more space. Yet there is disquieting power and prescience in Herbert's vision of the hive; it is a right-now-no-nictitating-allowed version of what we may make of ourselves with a combination of genetic engineering and behavior modification. *Hellstrom's Hive* belongs on the shelf with your other dystopias.

Major Characters:
  Trova Hellstrom: originator of hive, her "Words of the brood mother" guide the experiment.
  Nils Hellstrom: guiding genius of the hive.
  Carlos Depeaux: the first agency investigator we meet in the novel. Destroyed by Fancy.
  Tymiena: Depeaux's partner.
  Shorty Janvert: truncated agency investigator who serves as outsider "hero."
  Clovis Carr: Shorty's partner.
  Dzule Peruge: agency investigator who is as much the adversary of Merrivale as of the hive.
  Merrivale: fatuous, corrupt chief of investigation.
  Fancy Kalotermi: hypersexual hive female.
  Saldo: bright young hive executive in training.

The Godmakers

The Godmakers is part detective entertainment and part metaphysical essay. "The Continuing Adventures of Lewis Orne," as about one-third of the book might be called, follows the shrewd detecting of Lewis Orne, an ectype of one of Herbert's favorite characters. Orne is a redheaded genius who works within the system to solve insoluble problems. His close cousins are Ensign Ramsey (*Under Pressure*) and Jorj X. McKie (*Whipping Star*). During the remaining two-thirds of the book, he is the metaphysical adventurer who explores the dimensions of his own soul, as does Gilbert Dasein (*The Santaroga Barrier*) in a minor way and as do Paul and Leto II Atreides (*Dune* series) in depth.

Both the entertainment and the essay fit easily enough into the dominant paradigm of stressed homeostasis that is perhaps Herbert's *idee fixe*. The alternating pulse of the universe is, in the fictional present, returning from near-chaos toward its opposite limit, stasis. In the novel's historical past, the pan-sentient community has been all but destroyed by a series of "Rim Wars" that have left innumerable planets isolated and forgotten. Two organizations try to put things back in order: R&R (Rediscovery and Reeducation) seeks out isolated planets and provides the technological expertise required to bring them back to the level of galactic community: I-A (Investigation and Adjustment) checks the rediscovered planets for signs of war potential. If a planet is found to be war-like, an occupation force descends and stamps out either the tendency or the population. Together, R&R and I-A form a version of the complementary bureaus of other Herbert entertainments: BuPsych and BuSab. But at the present stage their tactical roles are reversed. R&R upsets the microstasis of isolated planets by prompting technological evolution, and I-A stomps out the cancerous order of war potential in the name of macro-order. Both wish to avoid the turmoil and disjunction of continued rim wars.

Orne has three narrated and one summarized "adventures." He unmasks the totalitarian reality beneath a planet's pastoral exterior. He awes a race of alien, simian glassblowers who aggressively attack the R&R. And we are told that he penetrates the nefarious intent of a matriarchal planet. This last adventure in planet-detecting nearly kills him, and he spends time in a crechpod, regrowing an eye, several limbs, and his guts. When he is reborn from the chrechpod, he battles a Bene-Gesserit-like conspiracy within the body politic. Each tale is well-paced, tensions are considerable, and the reader shares his hero's triumph. Orne's character and situation are ideal for a commercial author. Surely there are endless planets to be rediscovered, reeducated, investigated and adjusted. The adventurous Orne has all the qualities of Edgar Rice Burroughs' John Carter and Harry Harrison's Kerk Pyruus (*Deathworld*). An imagination so fertile as Herbert's could have gone on and on.

But Orne's adventurous entertainments give way to a more serious metaphysical essay. From the opening of the book, Orne has been subject to proleptic, symbolic dreams. And all the while he is adventuring, psi forces, radiating from the god-planet, Amal, where all religions have their center, seek him out. Each adventure fulfills a part of the psi prophecy, and Orne is incrementally prepared for metaphysical growth. The entertainment and essay are joined, perhaps clumsily, when Amal announces that it will oppose the continuation of I-A. Orne is sent by I-A to investigate at the same time that he is called to Amal to be the subject of the final phase of an experiment in godmaking. (The plot is repeated in *Dosadi*.) We discover that Orne is that rarest of things, a "psi focus." (Christ and Mohammed are previous cases: the one a god, the other a prophet.) From this point on, the entertaining adventures are decorative as the reader is invited to consider the relationships between self and Self, between I and Thou, between created and Creator. All of the empirical adjusting of structures in the name of homeostasis fades into insignificance as we follow Orne through the ordeals and temptations of discovering his Real Self. Orne's god-birth is something of a synthesis of the mystical elements of the *Dune* trilogy.

Perhaps the larger implications of *The Godmakers* have to do with escaping the dead-end of empirical manipulation so sharply revealed in *Hellstrom's Hive*. Man must turn inward, not outward; the future lies not in physics, but in metaphysics. Herbert hints that, at some point, the first is a minor province of the second. *Soul Catcher* is an investigation of this idea.

The Godmakers, however, is trapped by its element of adventure and, hence, concludes as an entertainment must. Orne integrates I-A with R&R; domesticates the matriarchal, Nathian conspiracy; and goes off on a honeymoon with the Nathianite, Diane Bullone, who is another version of Rhin Kelly (*The Green Brain*); Although Orne is demonstrably a god, he asserts that a honeymoon is what any red-blooded man would want. As a god, he cuts the gordian knot of finitude by promising man an open-ended account in the Bank of Time. Since anything can happen, endlessly, man never need confront his terminus. It's a big galaxy out there, and there are many other galaxies just next door.

Much of *The Godmakers* is lifted from *Dune*, but Herbert in simplifying the metaphysics has also vitiated its power. And the graphic, representative details of plot, setting, and character that make of *Dune* a complete world are insufficiently set forth in *The Godmakers*. The *scenes* are vividly realized, the *acts* are shadowy, and the *play* fails to take form. Herbert is not, here, at his best, but he is still very good.

Major Characters:

> Lewis Orne: R&R, I-A operative, runaway scion of a family involved in the Nathian conspiracy, psi-focus who becomes a god for the good of man.
>
> Umbo Stetson: I-A chief operative who plays Oscar Goldman to Orne's Colonel Austin.
>
> Polly Bullone: wife of Ipscott Bullone, High Commissioner; she heads the Nathian conspiracy.
>
> Diane Bullone: sweetheart and putative wife of Orne.
>
> Halmyrach, Abbod of Amal: high priest of psi who calls Orner to his godmaking.
>
> Bakrish: guru who leads Orne through god-ordeals.

Soul Catcher

The distinction between "entertainment" (in which the play among formulae articulates an idea) and "essay" (in which an idea forces articulation of form) is a matter of dominant tendency, rather than absolute category. Even the most formulaic of Herbert's stories bears the mark of his questing for the future of man. So, too, *Soul Catcher* employs plot devices, narrative displacements, and setting-as-character in ways familiar to readers of Herbert's ten previous novels. Yet *Soul Catcher* is an anomaly in Herbert's canon. Only *The Santaroga Barrier* has so "real" a setting in time and place: no aliens, no technological marvels, no time fractures. And *Soul Catcher* does not even have the "Jaspers Effect" which forms Santaroga's displacement. The basic narrative of *Soul Catcher* is less strange than Charles Manson's or Patty Hearst's story. Since there are no breaks in ontological verisimilitude, *Soul Catcher* qualifies as neither science fiction nor fantasy, and Herbert's casual readers are hence likely to be both disappointed and puzzled. Bantam, in seeking a marketing category, placed it in a list of books by or about American minority groups! With *Soul Catcher* Herbert has abandoned, temporarily, the conversation with Isaac Asimov, Larry Niven, and Eugene Zamiatin and rasied his voice in quite different company: Joesph Conrad, Franz Kafka, and William Faulkner.

The risk in this switch is enormous, for Herbert has not yet the powerful voice to clear his own space in the rhetorical world of major writers, but neither is he hopelessly out of his league. The giants may not listen very hard, but nobody need be embarrassed at Herbert's presumption. Herbert has always been master of creating fictional space. On occasion, one or more of his characters has stepped forward into four-dimensional reality; and from *Under Pressure* on, Herbert's fictions reveal his love-hate relationship with Humanity that all great novelists share.

Soul Catcher does not add to Herbert's earlier novels in the sense of being something new; rather, it strips away the buffers and props that assured his success in the world of science fiction, fantasy, and detective fiction. What remains is essential Herbert, without play or pretense. Gone is the paraphernalia that has allowed critics to dismiss Herbert as "escapist." Not, let me hasten to add, that there is no strangeness in *Soul Catcher*. Herbert's forest lifts us farther from our diurnal selves than does Ray Bradbury's Mars. But the strangeness of *Soul Catcher* is neither technological nor mystical; perhaps it might be best described as the realm of the "preternatural," as Francis (*A Canticle for Leibowitz*) discovers his world to be: something in between.

Soul Catcher may be summarized in a single sentence: a crazed Indian kidnaps a thirteen-year-old boy, drags him through the wilds of a national forest for two weeks, and then kills him. But this is to recognize only two of the four major characters in the novel: David Marshall and Charles Hobuhet. The straight-ahead reader is given plenty of ground for such a reading: Hobuhet's sister has committed suicide after being gang-raped; he has studied the demise of his people until he is ready for a Ph.D. in frustration and shame;

the abuses to which he has subjected his body could plausibly induce schizophrenia and hallucination. Those in the novel who give credence to his claims of spiritual power are themselves only a generation or two removed from the neolithic age. David is only a thirteen year-old who has been subjected to all the brain-washing necessary to produce a classic hostage syndrome. The few "supernatural" events—ravens and lightning appearing on cue—do not strain coincidence. Hobuhet's woodsmanship combined with David's terror and ignorance could easily account for the boy's inability to escape Hobuhet's maze. Read on this level, Bantam Books is right: *Soul Catcher* is a sensitive and disturbing plea for the original inhabitants of our land, an essay in "Red Power." The novel is the message Hobuhet wishes to send to all "hoquats."

But there are two other major characters: Katsuk and Hoquat. These two "projections' of Charles and David would, in other works of Herbert, be reified. In realistic fiction, they would remain the projections of a sick mind. In *Soul Catcher*, Katsuk and Hoquat are neither real nor illusory. Rather, they form a spiritual bridge between David and Charles and between the humans and the world of myth. The easiest way to undersand mythic reality is to invert existential reality. Mythic man exists only in so far as he repeats, in time, the atemporal action of a god. In myth, to be unique is to lose all reality. All "real" events have taken place, are taking place, and will take place. Mythic man's goal is to share in reality by ritual repetition of a god's act. All else is illusion.

One way to understand the dimensions of tragedy is to see it as the dislocation between the perception of myth and the achievement of history. The god-making of Lewis Orne, or of Leto II, is impossible in *Soul Catcher*. As it is for Ernest Hemingway's macho version ("The Short Happy Life of Francis McComer"), for Joseph Conrad's Kurtz (*Heart of Darkness*), and for William Faulkner's Thomas Sutpen (*Absalom, Absalom*). Kafka's Joseph K (*The Trial*) is literary first-cousin to David-Hoquat. Only when existential man deserts his ego can he share in supra-reality, but that sharing risks his empirical reality.

Thus, *Soul Catcher* has a large and available context, but it is not provided, directly, by Herbert's other fictions. In fact, knowing Herbert's usual methods may get in the way; however, knowing *Soul Catcher* is excellent preparation for perceiving Paul Atreides (*Dune*). *Soul Catcher* should be read in tandem with *The Godmakers* and *The Jesus Incident*, for all these books turn their backs on technological and genetic evolution in favor of man's search for at least one of the twenty-seven portals of the soul. The ironies of Kurt Vonnegut's *Sirens of Titan* reveal a similar conclusion. It is the fullness of life, not its duration, by which success should be judged. David-Hoquat's achievement in the two weeks he spends with Katsuk marks a life richly spent.

Two final points may be made. First, Herbert's spirit world is dependent upon belief: gods without worshippers wither, for creature and creator are, like everything else, symbiotic. Second, Charles Hobuhet misunderstands. Katsuk's arrow, composed of twentieth-century cedar and neolithic flint, does indeed complete a cycle of violation and retribution, but the cycle is both permanent and evanescent. Uncle Ish is not going to pick up the torch, and Katsuk's "message" to the white world will not be understood by David's mother. Charles is profoundly wrong: the significance of the ordeal and ritual slaying is limited to those performing the ritual. Mary Kletnik's rejection of her spirit self, Tskanny, is final.

We can no longer accept choral summations with grace; they sound preachy and intrusive. But King Lear's son-in-law, Edgar, assesses a much greater tragedy and triumph in words that might fit a full reading of *Soul Catcher*.

> The weight of this sad time we must obey,
> Speak what we feel, not what we ought to say.
> The oldest hath borne most: we that are young
> Shall never see so much, nor live so long.

In a curious way, *Soul Catcher* is a first novel. I hope there is a second to follow.

Major Characters:

Charles Hobuhet: crazed Indian who fancies himself the agent of vengeance on the white world.

Katsuk: latent spirit of Hobuhet, awakened by Bee, and served by Raven, who draws all to its center from which reality radiates.

David Marshall: thirteen year-old son of an undersecretary of state, who is kidnapped, led about for two weeks in the wilds of Washington, and then killed with an arrow.

Hoquat: latent spirit of David Marshall, called into being as complement of Katsuk.

The Dosadi Experiment

The Dosadi Experiment is cast as a sequel to *Whipping Star* (1970). Saboteur Extraordinary Jorj X. McKie moves among Calabans, Gowachins, Wreaves, Pan Spechi, Palenki, Chithers, Soborips, Laclacs, Taprisots, and various stripes of humans in his service to the Con Sentiency. Mercifully, we meet only Gowachin frog-people, Wreave mantis-people, and a Calaban or two. Other races are to be taken on faith as spear-carriers in the cosmic opera. McKie still travels through jumpdoors, communicates via sniggertrance, sits on chairdogs; and he is still the brightest mind ever to come down the galactic road. But he is incomplete because he has never been able to make a single one of his marriages work. This time, however, Herbert has given him a female counterpart. On the hellish planet, Dosadi, lives Keila Jedrik, the end product of a selective breeding scheme of the underground. She is part mentat, part Bene Gesserit, but she thinks herself sexually unattractive.

The boy-meets-girl plot is one of several; we watch the two haploids fall in love and achieve a Heinlein syzygy (*Fear No Evil*) by means of a blackbox-Gowachin-sybil-in-a-forcefield-bottle. Jung's somber model is burlesqued, for McKie and Jedrik can exchange bodies and communicate telepathically. As the chauvinist in Herbert would have it, Jedrik sacrifices herself, and McKie discovers that his body contains both personalities, both minds, and both sets of memories. The Jedrik-McKie kwisatz haderach sets out to do something unspecified to or for the universe as the book ends.

A second plot is equally vintage Herbert: the frog-like Gowachin have discovered that stress and pain push individuals and races toward their full potentials. Rather than leaving the universe to provide the crucibles for progress, a cabal of highly placed Gowachin officials (with human and Pan Spechi allies) has set up an experiment. Choosing a poison planet, the cabal has tricked Gowachin and Human settlers to emigrate—and then erased their memories. The planet stresses all but the strongest to destruction, and the plotters achieve serial ego immortality by transferring their egos into choice Dosadi bodies. Worn out bodies and the unwilling Dosadi selves are destroyed. The nefarious scheme is hidden and enabled by an iron-clad contract with a Calaban who provides a godwall around Dosadi, epiphanic-like communication with Dosadi puppet leaders, and ego transfers.

But the wily Dosadi do not remain passive victims, and since they have been honed into superbeings, the whole thing is getting out of hand. The Gowachin plotters call in McKie in hopes that he will precipitate something that will give them an excuse to sterilize Dosadi without public blame. Boy-meets-girl and hunter-becomes-hunted plots fuse as Jedrik and McKie become community. *Dosadi* is very much Herbert-revisited, carrying about as much punch as *The Eyes of Heisenberg*. The reader is left to decide for himself whether the immoral experiment on uninformed sentients is to be condemned or whether the boost given nature in forming man-plus is to be applauded. The sophisticated distinction between individual sexuality and the macro-forces of male and female, which seemed to emerge in *Children of Dune*, is blurred. Despite her brilliant exterior, Jedrik turns out to be a stereotyped woman, desiring to be help-meet to a sexually potent (but tender) man.

A third component of *Dosadi* gives credence to the assertion that it is a sequel to *Whipping Star*, if not in theme, character, or action, at least in gamesmanship. McKie is equipped as a Gowachin lawyer, and the most interesting parts of the novel concern his intricate legal dancing in the Gowachin Courtarena. Herbert gets in several potshots at our legal system, but since Herbert invents a new loophole every time McKie is about to lose, the reader is rather like a mark playing poker with a sharpie who keeps inventing new rules as the game progresses. For the reader who enjoys games in which constitutive rules are evolved by play, *Dosadi* provides some head music. Overall, *The Dosadi Experiment* is a potboiler by a talented author who must already have many pots—each with two chickens cooking.

Major Characters:
  Jorj X. McKie: BuSab operative, Gowachin lawyer, incompetent husband. Investigates Dosadi.
  Keila Jedrik: Dosadian super-woman, bred to break out from the planet. McKie's lover.
  Bildoon: Pan Spechi chief of BuSab.
  Ceyland: Wreave female Gowachin lawyer, McKie's deadly adversary in court.

Aritch: High Magister Gowachin, tries to use McKie to defuse his mess.
Broey: Gowachin on Dosadi, rival of Keila.

The Jesus Incident

Although *The Jesus Incident* is cast as a sequel to *Destination: Void*, it is not just the further adventures of Lord Tin Egg. The theme is the relationship beween self (individual ego) and Self (collective life). This favorite Herbert theme is played against a familiar ground: the nature of power and its effects on those who would seize it. The action progresses by means of a parallel series of maturations whose dialectic is between the male power of taking and the female power of yielding. And the basic question addressed is "What next, homo sapiens?" Thus *Incident* might be read as a sequel to several novels. The god, Ship, might have been the Green Brain, or Hive consciousness, or Lewis Orne (*Godmakers*), or Leto-Sandworm. *Incident* differs from its antecedents in a signal way: whereas *The Green Brain, Hellstrom's Hive, The Godmakers*, the *Dune* trilogy, and *Destination: Void* detail the gestation of gods, *The Jesus Incident* examines the boredom and frustration of a god whose creatures have for centuries disappointed Him. The burning Christian question, "What shall a man do to be saved?" has been modified into "How shall man Wor-ship?"

The time lapse between *Destination: Void* and *Incident* is vast. Ship has played and replayed history through many eons, watching men evolve until their suns burn out. On occasion Ship has interferred, unleashing the terrible power for love and destruction we know as the Crucifixion. But always His creatures have failed to discover what god requires. As each sun goes nova, Ship has gathered a few survivors and begun again. Sometimes the script has been run in Eden, sometimes in sheol, often in the kind of twilight land in which we live. Herbert's latest novel is the story of one last effort by Ship to grant His creatures responsible free will. If the music fails to come out right *this* time, Ship promises to break the record—to abandon man altogether.

Rather than the Eden provided man at the end of *Void*, Ship has given man a planet called Pandora. It is a curious and dreadful place, compounded of Dosadi, Harry Harrison's Deathworld, and H.G. Wells' Island of Dr. Moreau. Demons of every nightmare variety—from Nerve Runners to Hooded Dashers to Spinnerets—prey upon the colonists. Humanity's every effort is directed to short term survival and long term sterilization of the planet. As in *The Eyes of Heisenberg*, a triumvirate runs man's affairs: Morgan Oakes is the Chaplain/Psychiatrist, who has taken complete power; Jesus Lewis is the Frankenstein dabbling in recombinant mutation; and Sy Murdoch is their sadistic muscle-man. Each of the three is composed of several stock characters: Oakes is the consummate evil politician; Lewis is the amoral scientist; and Murdoch is the handsome, civilized commandant of a Nazi laboratory. But Oakes is also the rebel against a paternalistic god, Lewis is the devil, and Murdoch his own most pathetic victim.

Since it is obvious that whatever independence from Ship Oakes and company achieve will not be devoted to developing "the best of their own humanity," Ship starts a second group of actors. He awakens Raja Flattery (the CeePee from the Tin Egg who helped awaken Ship) from hybernation, discovers and trains a poet (Kerro Panille), and transports a voluptuous medtech (Hali Ekel) back to Golgotha where she, in the body of an old woman, witnesses the crucifixion. Two other women complete the cast of major, human characters. Waela TaoLini is a beautiful Pandoran woman whose skin changes colors to reflect her emotional state. Legata Hamill is a "pocket Venus" with "doll face" and "green eyes," who has the strength of six men. Both Pandoran ladies have been produced by Jesus Lewis' genetic experiments.

The dominant life form on Pandora is not the host of nightmare predators but rather Electrokelp. The kelp is communally sentient, naming itself "Avata"—the ancient superego of the Hindu oversoul. One of its vectors is the "hylighters," hydrogen filled bags that cruise the air like Portuguese men-o-war. Oakes decides that the 'lectrokelp is the real enemy and sets Lewis the task of destroying it. Meanwhile, Waela, Kerro and Raja (renamed Thomas, the doubter) attempt to communicate with the kelp by diving into its midst in a submarine equipped to play back the winking lights by which the kelp is thought to communicate.

Oakes has sabotaged the sub, and the three are saved by hylighters whose presence acts as a powerful hallucinogen. Kerro and Waela copulate while in contact with the hylighters, and the resulting fetus develops very rapidly. The experience links human minds into a kind of Tiggywaugh's web (*Heaven Makers*) which makes it possible to understand that all Ship ever wanted was for man to be the best he can.

The novel ends with the birth of a hybrid Avata and human, as a sort of female kwisatz haderach named Vata. Ship takes its devil Lewis, leaves Raja in exchange for Oakes, and sails off to construct new scenarios in the Holy Void. The electrokelp dies as a result of Lewis' manipulations, but, like Christ, it provides man with a fuller sense of his own potential. God's in His heaven, all is right with the world, but man has been weaned—in all ways—from the shiptits.

Among the many riches that flesh out *Incident* is Herbert's boldest exploitation of sex. Oakes lusts for Legata, Hali Ekel wants the poet's body, and Raja wants to bed Waela. The "scream room" presided over by Murdoch (initials S-M) is a *1984* horror where all sexual perversions are permitted or forced. The maitre-d' is a kindly hermaphrodite named Jessup who weeps as he groans in auto-coitus. Beside the portals stand two flesh flowers who cry "Feed me," and inside are full-grown bodies with infant minds and inexhaustible, sad potency: sweat, musk, mindless, drugged orgasm—a sense of terrible privation reminiscent of Cordwainer Smith's classic "A Planet Called Sheol." Legata Hamill allows Oakes to use her amazon body even though he has subjected her to the scream room. Herbert seems to use sex as metaphor for the tenet that only by knowing the worst can the best be understood.

Finally, as all novelists do, Herbert uses *Incident* to talk about writing a novel. The question Ship and Raja discuss is precisely relevant for an author who follows the same metaphysical questions in sequential books: Does a new book constitute merely a replay of a previous effort? Or does it continue and even correct its antecedents? *The Dosadi Experiment* reads like a worn and scratched record on a tired phonograph. But in *The Jesus Incident*, Herbert—like Ship—creates and then frees his characters. *Dosadi* is a read-once-and-dispose. *Incident* requires, and rewards, several readings.

On the other hand, the technical skill of *Incident* wavers. For example, one way to get character description over quickly is to allow the character to examine himself in a mirror—but it's a primitive technique. *Incident* uses it over and over. Certainly allusion through names can enrich both texture and context, but somehow the author shouldn't tell us that a character named *Pan*ille is Pan-like. Herbert establishes numerous ironic juxtapositions of character and event, but he might have trusted his reader to spot them without such obvious proddings.

Yet there are patches of lyric power, painfully tactile scenes, exuberant action shots, and empathic dark-nights-of-the-psyche. With the exception of Jesus Lewis, the villains are painted in shades of gray, rather than in melodramatic black. Raja Thomas is a useful Herbert persona. And of the heroes, only Kerro Panille seems constantly in danger of riding off on a white horse. Perhaps *Incident* can lead the hypertrophied fan toward an understanding of the sophistications of main-stream technique, and it may even tempt the literary snob toward science fiction. Something, or someone has reenergized Herbert. Perhaps we are indebted to Bill Ransom.

Major Characters:
>Ship: the artificial intelligence who has awakened as a god.
>
>Avata: the sentient kelp who is sacrificed to allow man-plus to be born.
>
>Raja Thomas (Flattery): CeePee from *Destination: Void* whom Ship thrusts into Pandora as a catalyst.
>
>Morgan Oakes: would-be atheist CeePee who wishes to build a material paradise and is quite willing to break many eggs in the process.
>
>Jesus Lewis: devil in human (scientist) form who builds people and monstrosities with indifference.
>
>Hali Ekel: shipwoman sent back to view the Crucifixion.
>
>Winslow Ferry: decadent, lecherous ship surgeon.
>
>Waela TaoLini: mother of Vata by Kerro Panille and Avata.
>
>Kerro Panille: poet who links with Avata and leads man to community.
>
>Legata Hamill: super-strong beautiful woman who accepts degradation without being degraded.

V

SHORT STORIES

The Worlds of Frank Herbert

The Book of Frank Herbert

Most of Herbert's short stories were either chunks of a novel in progress or seeds for future novels. A fascinating study might be made of the ways in which they grew into longer fictions. Of those not yet incorporated, nineteen are easily accessible in the two collections, published in 1971 and 1973, respectively. The earliest story ("Looking for Something," 1952) and the most recent ("Gambling Device," 1973) are strikingly alike in plotting, style, characterization, and theme. A hasty conclusion might be that in short fiction Herbert works quickly, confidently, and within formulae he very early found to be successful. A more careful consideration might yield the same impression.

Many of the stories fit in the category of "detective science fiction." Jorj X. McKie ("The Tactful Saboteur"), Welby Lewis ("Rat Race"), Varley Trent ("Gone Dogs"), Eric Ladde ("Operation Syndrome"), Ivar Norris Gump ("By the Book"), and Bill Custer ("Committee of the Whole") are pretty much the same character, despite their obvious surface differences. Each brings his special abilities to bear, each is an intelligent maverick tolerated despite eccentricities; each is driven by an almost Ayn Rand sense of enlightened selfishness. And each, coincidentally, saves the situation. Beneath hard exteriors, they are romantic softies: Trent is a fool for dogs; Custer sees all men as giants; Ladde falls for a torch-singer. Thus the super-brain is humanized. The formula is sure-fire for light fiction because the reader knows whom to side with and shares in the triumph of the under-dog. Since the character and the problem are tailored for each other, plot and character evolve simultaneously without distracting complexity, and the stories end with a warm glow.

Herbert picks up some of the characters for his longer fictions, even when he does not make use of individual stories. Jorj X. McKie ("The Tactful Saboteur") reappears in *Whipping Star* and again in *The Dosadi Experiment* although in Dosadi he is in danger of becoming a three dimensional character. Eric Ladde ("Operation Syndrome") becomes the crew and the captain too of *Destination: Void*.

Female characters are also typical. Marie Medill ("Mating Call") and Gwen Everest ("A-W-F Unlimited") are liberated women who really want a man. Their respective foils (Laconia Wilkinson and General Sonnet Finnister) are dried-up-man-eaters who dimly suspect that they need a man, a pegnoir, and a bed. Herbert's short fiction is thoroughly male-chauvinist-pig—like most science fiction.

Herbert's aliens turn out to have very human problems: Panthor Bolin, Pan-Spechi of "Tactful Saboteur," is a prude; so is Gafka, the Rukuchp of

"Mating Call." The aliens in "Escape Felicity" can't keep the undesirables out of the neighborhood. "The Featherbedders" shows aliens acting out the human struggle between bureaucrats and free riders. The super beings of "Old Rambling House" can't keep help in a boring job. The aliens who conduct the experiment in "Rat Race" find their subjects getting lab wise. The Vegans of "The Gone Dogs" are cursed with an oriental sense of "face."

Two of the collected stories break sharply from Herbert's usual formula short story. "Seed Stock" is a sensitive story of man's misguided, and therefore doomed, efforts to modify an alien environment to fit himself, rather than allowing himself to mutate so as to fit the environment. Only the chief character, Kroudar, allows his biological mind to make proper adjustments. Kroudar is miles from the brilliant, detective misfit we expect in one guise or another. "Seed Stock" reads very like the beginning of a Herbert novel.

"Passage for Piano," despite its punning title, weighs the human value of music against more practical values. The colonists take the guts of a ton-and-a-half Steinway to their new world instead of personal articles or more support materials. Had they given up something really important, perhaps even crucial to survival on the new world, "Passage for Piano" might also make the first chapter of a novel. The twelve-year-old musical genius, blind and linked to his grandfather, might constitute a variation on Paul (*Dune*).

On balance, the stories Herbert has chosen for reprinting are entertainments: predictable, wry, witty, and dominated by formulae. Many of them would not be out of place in collections of entertainments by other science-fiction writers. "The Nothing" would fit in Robert A. Heinlein's "Rolling Stones" collection. "The Gone Dogs" would work in Clifford Simak's *City*. And "By the Book" might have been written by Isaac Asimov.

But. The formulaic quality of Herbert's short fiction is not really a fault. Rather, the two collections of stories testify to the skill and effort Herbert expended in mastering his genre. Entertainments are supposed to be formula fiction. The reader who demands something more is merely in the wrong pew.

VI

ANNOTATED PRIMARY BIBLIOGRAPHIES

I. Novels

Children of Dune. New York: Berkley/Putnam, 1976.
   This third volume of the *Dune* trilogy follows the maturation of Paul's twins, Leto and Ghanima, within the storm center of the known universe, the planet Arrakis. Contending forces, from the little makers to the heirs of the Imperium, test Leto. All are absorbed into Herbert's most fully developed man-plus.

Destination: Void. New York: Berkley, 1966.
   A skeleton crew of clones must develop a super artificial brain to run their space ship, the *Tin Egg*, or die. Their success produces a literal *deus ex machina*. *The Jesus Incident* is a sequel.

The Dosadi Experiment. New York: Berkley/Putnam, 1977.
   Jorj X. McKie, Saboteur Extraordinary, is sent to investigate an illegal "sress-planet" set up by a Gowachin cabal in order to produce superior bodies into which their egos can be transferred. *Dosadi* is a sequel to *Whipping Star*, which is a sequel to "The Tactful Saboteur" (1964).

The Dragon in the Sea. Garden City, NY: Doubleday, 1956. Later titles: *21st Century Sub* (1956); *Under Pressure* (1974).
   Herbert's first published novel describes the adventure-investigation-maturation of Ensign Ramsey, undercover man from BuPsych. The *Fenian Ram's* mission is to steal crude oil from the enemy's continental shelf.

Dune. Philadelphia: Chilton, 1965.
   Volume one of the *Dune* trilogy traces the development through stress assimilation of Paul Atreides, heir to the noblest feudal house in the universe. He absorbs the Bene Gesserit plan, becomes a mentat, becomes the Fremen's messiah-god, defeats the Harkonnen and the Imperium and mounts the throne, hoping to avert a bloody jihad.

Dune Messiah. New York: Berkley, 1969.
   Volume two of the *Dune* trilogy picks up Paul's problems as emperor —after the jihad. Various plotters (from his wife to the super-scientific Tleilaxu) try to pull Paul down or control him. Paul fights an interior battle against the forces of memory and prescience to maintain his humanity and free will.

The Eyes of Heisenberg. New York: Berkley, 1966.

In a world divided between two hideous classes of super humans, Optimen and Cyborgs, a nuclear family struggles to maintain itself to produce a child.

The Godmakers. New York: Putnam, 1972.
Lewis Orne travels about the universe watching for signs of aggressiveness in emerging cultures. He is selected to become a god by the priests of psi, and does so, through stress, death, and rebirth.

The Green Brain. New York: Ace, 1966.
The insect population, nearly wiped out by man, fights back by developing a super brain. Investigators discover that animals, plants, and insects are symbiotic, and that inter-kingdom symbiosis is the next evolutionary step.

The Heaven Makers. New York: Avon, 1968.
All the world is a stage for the man-plus Chem who have manipulated human history in order to film entertainments for themselves. Klexel, a Chem, is sent to check for illegalities in the filming operation. Dr. Thurlow, a human, is immune to the Chem's invisibility devices. Both "love" the same woman.

Hellstrom's Hive (Project 40). Garden City, NY: Nelson Doubleday [Science Fiction Book Club], 1973.
A new culture, based upon the bee model, develops in an ultra-normal rural setting. Investigators are killed, enslaved, or co-opted. The hive moves toward direct confrontation with a decadent America.

The Jesus Incident. New York: Berkley, 1979. Written with Bill Ransom.
In this sequel to *Destination: Void*, the god, Ship, has tired of man's inability to find a proper way of wor-ship. Humanity is given one last chance on a nightmare planet. Raja Flattery (from *Void*) is awakened. Among Ship's stress experiments is the crucifixion of Jesus.

The Santaroga Barrier. New York: Berkley, 1968.
A California valley shows great sales resistance, a good-old-days America, and extraordinary clanishness. An investigator, Gilbert Dasein, is almost killed by the valley's collective mind, but through a mind-expanding drug, Jaspers, becomes a Santarogan.

Soul Catcher. New York: Putnam, 1972.
An American Indian, driven to the breaking point by racial shame and the gang rape of his sister, is instructed by a god to capture, test, and execute an innocent white man. He captures the young son of a government official; the two spend their last two weeks in our western mountains.

Whipping Star. New York: Putnam, 1970.

Jorj X. McKie, Saboteur Extraordinary, must solve the mystery of the disappearing Calabans before the consentiency is destroyed. Fanny Mae, the star-gate Calaban, falls in love with McKie, and together they solve the problems of non-referential language sufficiently to defeat the kinky Mliss Abnethe who is behind the universe's problem.

II. Short Stories

A. Collections of Herbert by Herbert

The Worlds of Frank Herbert, New York: Ace, 1971.

Title	Original Publication
"A-W-F, Unlimited"	*Galaxy*, June 1961.
"By the Book"	*Astounding/Analog SF*, August 1966.
"Committee of the Whole"	*Galaxy*, April 1965.
"Escape Felicity"	*Astounding/Analog SF*, June 1966.
"The Featherbedders"	*Astounding/Analog SF*, August 1967.
"The GM Effect"	*Astounding/Analog SF*, June 1965.
"Mating Call"	*Galaxy*, October 1961.
"Old Rambling House"	*Galaxy*, April 1958.
"The Tactful Saboteur"	*Galaxy*, October 1964.

The Book of Frank Herbert. New York: Daw Books, 1973.

"Encounter in a Lonely Place"	(new)
"Gambling Device"	(new)
"The Gone Dogs"	*Amazing Stories*, November 1954.
"Looking for Something?"	*Startling Stories*, April 1952.
"The Nothing"	*Fantastic Universe*, January 1956.
"Occupation Force"	*Fantastic*, August 1955.
"Operation Syndrome"	*Astounding/Analog SF*, June 1954.
"Passage for Piano"	(new)
"Rat Race"	*Astounding/Analog SF* July 1955.
"Seed Stock"	*Astounding/Analog SF*, April 1970.

B. Collection of Herbert by editor

The Best of Frank Herbert. Ed. Angus Wells. London: Sidgwick and Jackson, 1975.

"The Being Machine"	*IF, Worlds of SF*, October 1969.
"By the Book"	*Astounding/Analog SF*, August 1966.
"Committee of the Whole"	*Galaxy*, April 1965.
"Dragon in the Sea"	*Astounding/Analog SF*, November 1955.
"Dune" ("Dune World")	Chilton version of 1965; Originally published in *Astounding/Analog SF*, December 1963.
"Egg and Ashes"	*IF, Worlds of SF*, November 1960.
"The Heaven Makers"	*Amazing Stories— Amazing SF*, April 1967.
"Nightmare Blues" ("Operation Syndrome")	*Astounding/Analog SF*, June 1954.
"The Primitives"	*Galaxy*, April 1966.
"Cease Fire"	*Astounding/Analog SF*, January 1958.
"Seed Stock"	*Astounding/Analog SF*, April 1970.

C. Collections including Herbert

"A-W-F, Unlimited" (*Galaxy*, June 1961)	*17 X Infinity*. Ed. Groff Conklin. New York: Dell, 1963.
"Carthage: Reflections of a Martian" (poem)	*Mars, We Love You*. Ed. Hipolito and McNelly. New York: Doubleday, 1971.
"Cease Fire" (*Astounding/Analog SF*, January 1958)	*A Century of Science Fiction*. Ed. Damon Knight. New York: Simon and Schuster, 1962
"Committee of the Whole" (*Galaxy*, April 1965)	*Science Fiction Inventions*. Ed. Damon Knight. New York: Lancer, 1967.
"Death of a City" (new)	*Future City*. Ed. Roger Elwood. New York: Trident, 1973.
"Egg and Ashes" (*IF, Worlds of SF*, November 1960).	*The Best Science Fiction from IF*. Ed. Frederick Pohl. New York: *Galaxy* 1964.
"The Featherbedders" (*Astounding/Analog SF*,	*Analog 7*. Ed. John W. Campbell, Jr. New York:

August 1967).

"Greenslaves"
   (*Amazing Stories–Amazing SF*, March 1965)

"Greenslaves"
   (*Amazing Stories–Amazing SF*, March 1965)

"Looking for Something?"
   (*Startling Stories*, April 1952)

"The Mary Celeste Move"
   (*Astounding/Analog SF*, October 1964).

"The Mary Celeste Move"
   (*Astounding/Analog SF*, October 1964).

"Mating Call"
   (*Galaxy* October 1961).

"The Mind Bomb"
   ("The Being Machine," *IF, World of If*, October 1969).

"Missing Link"
   (*Astounding/Analog SF*, February 1959).

"Murder Will In"
   (*Magazine of Fantasy and Science Fiction*. May 1970)

"Nightmare Blues"
   (*Astounding/Analog SF*, June 1954).

"The Nothing"
   (*Fantastic Universe*, January 1956)

"The Primitives"
   (*Galaxy*, April 1966).

"Science Fiction and
a World in Crisis"
   (essay).

"Seed Stock"
   (*Astounding/Analog SF*, April 1970).

Doubleday, 1970.

On Our Way to the Future. Ed. Terry Carr. New York: Ace, 1970.

Bug-Eyed Monsters. Ed. Anthony Cheetham, London: Panther, 1974.

SF Yearbook: A Treasury of Science Fiction, November 1970.

Eco-Fiction. Ed. John Stadler. New York: Washington Square, 1971.

Analog 4. Ed. John W. Campbell, Jr. New York: Doubleday, 1966.

13 Above the Night. Ed. Groff Conklin. New York: Dell, 1965.

The Best from IF, Vol 1. Editors of *IF*. New York: Award, 1973.

SF: Authors' Choice. Ed. Harry Harrison. New York: Berkley, 1968.

Five Fates. Ed. Keith Laumer. New York: Double-day, 1970.

Best Science Fiction Stories and Novels. Ed. T.E. Dikty. New York: Fredrick Fell, 1955.

Tomorrow, and Tomorrow, and Tomorrow . . . . Ed. Bonnie Heintz, Frank Herbert, Donald Joos, and Jane McGee. New York: Holt, Rinehart and Winston, 1974.

The Tenth Galaxy Reader. Ed. Frederick Pohl. New York: Doubleday, 1967.

Science Fiction, Today and Tomorrow. Ed. Reginald Bretnor. New York: Harper & Row, 1974.

Nightmare Garden. Ed. Vic Ghidalia, New York: Manor, 1976.

"The Tactful Saboteur" (*Galaxy*, October 1964).	*Seven Trips Through Time and Space*. Ed. Groff Conklin. New York: Fawcett, 1968.
"Try to Remember!" (*Amazing Stories— Amazing SF*, October 1961).	*The Best of Amazing*. Ed. Joseph Ross. New York: Doubleday, 1967.

D. First appearance of story—listed chronologically

"Looking for Something?"	*Startling Stories* April 1952.
"Nightmare Blues" ("Operation Syndrome")	*Astounding/Analog SF*, June 1954.
"Pack Rat Planet"	*Astounding/Analog SF*, December 1954.
"Rat Race"	*Astounding/Analog SF*, July 1955.
"Operation Force"	*Fantastic*, August 1955.
"Dragon in the Sea" ("Under Pressure")	*Astounding/Analog SF*, November 1955; December 1955; January 1956.
"The Nothing"	*Fantastic Universe*, January 1956.
"Cease Fire"	*Astounding/Analog SF*, January 1958.
"Old Rambling House"	*Galaxy*, April 1958.
"You Take the High Road"	*Astounding/Analog SF*, May 1958.
"A Matter of Traces"	*Fantastic Universe*, November 1958.
"Missing Link"	*Astounding/Analog SF*, February 1959.
"Operation Haystack"	*Astounding/Analog SF*, May 1959.
"The Priests of Psi"	*Fantastic*, February 1960.
"Egg and Ashes"	*IF, Worlds of Science Fiction*, November 1960.
"A-W-F, Unlimited"	*Galaxy*, June 1961.
"Mating Call"	*Galaxy*, October 1961.
"Try to Remember!"	*Amazing Stories—Amazing Science Fiction*, October 1961.
"Mindfield"	*Amazing Stories—Amazing Science Fiction*, March 1962.
"Dune World"	*Astounding/Analog SF*, December 1963; January 1964; February 1964.
"The Mary Celeste Move"	*Astounding/Analog SF*, October 1964.
"The Tactful Saboteur"	*Galaxy*, October 1964.

"The Prophet of Dune"	*Astounding/AnalogSF*, January 1965; February 1965; March 1965; April 1965; May 1965.
"Greenslaves"	*Amazing Stories—Amazing SF*, March 1965.
"Committee of the Whole"	*Galaxy* April 1965.
"The GM Effect"	*Astounding/Analog SF*, June 1965.
"Do I Wake or Dream?"	*Galaxy*, August 1965.
"The Primitives"	*Galaxy*, April 1966.
"Escape Felicity"	*Astounding/Analog SF*, June 1966.
"Heisenberg's Eyes"	*Galaxy*, June 1966; August 1966.
"By the Book"	*Astounding/Analog SF*, August 1966.
"The Heaven Makers"	*Amazing Stories—Amazing SF*, April 1967; June 1967.
"The Featherbedders"	*Astounding/Analog SF*, August 1967.
"Santaroga Barrier"	*Amazing Stories—Amazing SF*, October 1967, December 1967; February 1968.
"Dune Messiah"	*Galaxy* July 1969; August 1969; September 1969; October 1969; November 1969.
"The Being Machine"	*IF, Worlds of Science Fiction*, January 1970; February 1970; March 1970; April 1970.
"Seed Stock"	*Astounding/Analog SF*, April 1970.
"Murder Will In"	*Fantasy and Science Fiction*, May 1970.

VII

ANNOTATED SECONDARY BIBLIOGRAPHY

Aldiss, Brian W. *Billion Year Spree: The True History of Science Fiction*. London: Weidenfeld & Nicolson, 1973.
  Lists Herbert among "giants'" but his admiration is temperate. Likes sensuous detail; notes interest in ecology.

Allen, L. David. *The Ballantine Teachers' Guide to Science Fiction*. New York: Ballantine, 1975, pp. 273-90.
  Discusses *Under Pressure* as a psychological novel.

_____ *Herbert's Dune and Other Works*. Lincoln, Nebraska: Cliffs Notes, 1975.
  Essays on *The Book of Frank Herbert* and *The Worlds of Frank Herbert* (collections). Major essays on *Dune* and *Dune Messiah*. Brief essays on *God Makers, Under Pressure, Destination: Void, Eyes of Heisenberg, Green Brain, Santaroga Barrier, Whipping Star*, and *Hellstrom's Hive*.
  Allen's is the most comprehensive study to date of Herbert; recommended.

Barron, Neil, Ed. *Anatomy of Wonder, Science Fiction*. New York and London: Bowker, 1976.
  Summaries of *Destination: Void; Dragon in the Sea (Under Pressure); Dune; Eyes of Heisenberg; Hellstrom's Hive (Project 40)*. Notes that California State at Fullerton has collection of Herbert manuscripts.

Bretnor, Reginald, ed. *The Craft of Science Fiction: A Symposium on Writing Science Fiction*. New York: Harper & Row, 1976.
  Passing references to *Dragon in the Sea* (pp. 96-97), *Dune* (pp. 139, 213, 289, 324), *God Makers* (pp. 81-82), and *Santaroga Barrier* (pp. 82-84).

Carter, Paul A. *The Creation of Tomorrow: Fifty Years of Magazine Science Fiction*. New York: Columbia University Press, 1977.
  Notes that *Dune* is the most popular of the past twenty years. Finds it "Curiously old fashioned." Links *Dune* with Burroughs' John Carter stories. Uses *Dune* as a bench mark.

Clareson, Thomas D., ed. *Many Futures, Many Worlds: Theme and Form in Science Fiction*. Kent, Ohio: Kent State University Press, 1977.
  Thomas L. Wymer, "Perception and Value in Science Fiction": *Dune* is sophisticated and honest exploration of free will in deterministic universe.
  Thomas D. Clareson, "Many Futures, Many Worlds": *Hellstrom's Hive* is literary Naturalism.
  Stanley Schmidt, "The Science in Science Fiction": Herbert can write hard-core science fiction.
  Patricia Warrick, "Images of the Man-Machine Intelligence Relationship in Science Fiction": *Destination: Void* is a responsible investigation of aritifical intelligence.

Gunn, James E. *Alternate Worlds: The Illustrated History of Science Fiction*.

Englewood Cliffs, N.J.: Prentice-Hall, 1975. In passing, pp. 30, 212, 239.

Hollister, Bernard C., and Deane C. Thompson. *Grokking the Future: Science Fiction in the Classroom*, Dayton, Ohio: Pflaum, 1973. *Dune* is "useful" in science fiction course.

Ketterer, David. *New Worlds for Old: The Apocalyptic Imagination, Science Fiction and American Literature*. Bloomington: Indiana University Press, 1974.

Herbert is apocalyptic and ecological author. Uses *Dune* as standard for judging Ursula K. LeGuin's *Left Hand of Darkness*.

Kroitor, Harry P. "The Special Demands of Point of View in Science Fiction." *Extrapolation*, 17 (1976), 153-59. Brief use of Herbert.

Manlove, C.N. *Modern Fantasy: Five Studies*. Cambridge: Cambridge University Press, 1975.

Excludes *Dune* from fantasy because it takes place in our universe and describes events that could happen.

Merrill, Judith. "Books," *The Magazine of Fantasy and Science Fiction*, March 1966, pp. 51-53.

Unfavorable review of *Dune*.

McClintock, Michael. "Some Preliminaries to the Criticism of Science Fiction." *Extrapolation*, 15 (1973), 17-24.

Moskowitz, Samuel. *Seekers of Tomorrow: Masters of Science Fiction*. Cleveland: World Publishing, 1966.

O'Reilly, Timothy. "From Concept to Fable: The Evolution of Frank Herbert's *Dune*." In *Critical Encounters*. Ed. Dick Riley. New York: Frederick Ungar, 1978. pp. 41-55.

Highly recommended. Assessment of *Dune's* literary and intellectual complexity.

Ower, John. "Idea and Imagery in Herbert's *Dune*." *Extrapolation*, 15 (1974), 129-39. Highly recommended.

Panshin, Alexei. *Science Fiction in Dimension: A Book of Explorations*. Chicago: Advent, 1976.

Finds Herbert powerful but awkward. Likes *Dragon in the Sea*. Labels *Dune* a melodrama of ecology and fanaticism. Thinks Herbert's other works aren't very good.

Parkinson, Robert C. "*Dune*—An Unfinished Tetralogy." *Extrapolation* 13 (1971), 16-24.

Remington, Thomas J. "Three Reservations on the Structural Road." Science-Fiction Studies, 4 (1977), 48-54.

Discussion of Scholes' *Structuralist Fabulation*. Critical of Scholes' condescension to Herbert.

Rothfork, John. "Grokking God: Phenomenology in NASA and Sci-Fi." *Research Studies*, 44 (1976), 101-110.

Religion and mythology in *Destination: Void*.

Sadoul, Jacques. *Histoire de la science-fiction moderne (1911-1971)*. Paris: Albin Michel, 1973.

Admires *Dune*, but finds it overly long. Likes *Dune Messiah* less.

Sanders, Scott. "Invisible Men and Women: The Disappearance of Characters in Sci-Fi." *Science-Fiction Studies*, 4 (1977), 14-24.

Brief discussion of Leto II (*Children of Dune*).

Scholes, Robert, and Eric S. Rabkin. *Science Fiction: History Science, Vision*. New York: Oxford University Press, 1977.

Dune is superior to *Foundation Trilogy*: Herbert creates a new mythology. Blends adventure and ecology.

Stover, Leon E. "Is Jaspers Beer Good for you? Mass Society and Counter Culture in Herbert's *Santaroga Barrier*." *Extrapolation*, 17 (May 1976), 160-67;

Sutton, Thomas C., and Marilyn Sutton. "Science Fiction as Mythology." *Western Folklore*. 28 (October 1969), 230-37;

Claims Herbert as visionary and mythographer.

INDEX

51, *54-56*
Jung, Carl, in *Dune*, 23, 24; in *Children of Dune*, 29, 30; in *The Dosadi Experiment*, 52 (see also Freud, Sigmund)

Kafka, Franz, 50, 51
King Lear (William Shakespeare), Edgar's final speech, 52

"Looking for Something?," 57

"Man-Plus," Ensign Ramsey in *Under Pressure*, 14; in *The Dosadi Experiment*, 53, in *The Jesus Incident*, 56; in *Children of Dune*, 59
"Mating Call," 57
Modes, Herbert's use of, comedic Bildungsroman, 29; detective fiction, 9, 50; divine comedy, 29; epic fantasy, 16; escapist, 16, 50; fantasy, 9, 50; heroic fantasy, 38; lab report, 38; mythic, 51, "preternatural," 50; realism, 9, 16, 51; science fiction, 9, 16, 33, 38, 41, 50, 56; sword-and-sorcery, 9, 16; tragedy, 29, 51

Niven, Larry, *Ringworld*, 32; 50
"Nothing, The," 58

"Old Rambling House," 58
"Operation Syndrome" ("Nightmare Blues"), 57

"Passage for Piano," 58

"Rat Race," 57, 58

Salinger, J. D., *Catcher in the Rye*, 15, 16
Santaroga Barrier, The, 9, 34, 37, 39, *41-43*, 45, 48, 50

"Seed Stock," 58
Self vs. self, 54 (see also Consciousness)
Setting (Secondary Universe), in *Dune*, 10, 18; in *Under Pressure, Dune, Soul Catcher*, 15; in *Children of Dune*, 29; in *Destination: Void*, 39; in *The Godmakers*, 49; in *Soul Catcher, Santaroga Barrier*, 50
Sheckley, Robert, "Specialist," 47
Simak, Clifford, *City*, 58
Smith, Cordwainer, 10
Soul Catcher, 9, 10, 15, 47, 49, *50-52*
Stapledon, Olaf, *Last and First Man*, 21

"Tactful Saboteur, The," 57
Themes, Herbert's favorite, Dynamic Homeostasis, 9 (see entry); Self vs. self, 54 (see also Consciousness)
Tolkien, J.R.R., *The Lord of the Rings*, 15, 16, 32

Under Pressure, 9, *14-15*, 34, 35, 36, 48, 50

Vonnegut, Kurt, *Sirens of Titan*, 39, 51

Wells, H.G., *The Island of Dr. Moreau*, 54
Whipping Star, 9, 28, *43-45*, 48, 52, 53, 57
Women, Herbert's attitude towards, in *Under Pressure*, 15; in *Children of Dune*, 29-31; in *The Green Brain*, 34-35; in *The Heaven Makers*, 40; in *Hellstrom's Hive*, 46-47; in *The Dosadi Experiment*, 52-53; in *The Jesus Incident*, 54-55; in "Mating Call," "A-W-F Unlimited," 57

Zamiatin, Eugene, 50
Zelazny, Roger, *Lord of Light*, 32